AF444802

Introduction

This book has evolved out of an academic course of English Language on which I taught, and that is still running as a required course for students of Political, International, Communication, and Social Studies at the School of Political Sciences (University of Florence), and as an option for students in other departments.

At the beginning of the course I assumed that my students were generally not specialists in the area of language study and linguistics, and therefore they needed an introduction to the kind of topics which are necessary for approaching the texts and conducting in-depth analysis. For this reason, two weeks of lessons covered some basic preliminaries of semantics, pragmatics, rhetoric, and strategies for persuasion, during which I also introduced, among others, Lakoff's theories and Van Dijk's account. Thus, each article in this book deals with topics that have been the subject of previous investigation in class and therefore theoretical background is mostly taken for granted and not explained further during the argumentation.

Ultimately, the book offers some examples of analyses of speeches uttered by very outstanding people of the worldwide scene on social and political subjects. I have maintained a focus on English (primarily British and American), while the selected speeches vary in many relevant respects, such as historical time, addresses and addressees, and the topic they deal with (economics, peace, war, society and so on). Nonetheless, they have a common denominator: the mutual relationship between language and ideology.

In fact, language is a source of evidence for people's conceptual systems. Language has a powerful role in establishing, maintaining and also changing system of ideas, beliefs and practises, and representations. In other words, our abstract system of values becomes actualized in language and, on the other hand, language contributes to shape it. Public speaking of very influencing people (not only politicians, but also economists, businessmen, singers, etc.) on formal occasions on community-related topics is a consciously constructed framework consisting of many linguistic devices aimed to explain, persuade or even manipulate our system of ideas and beliefs.

The central part of the book is composed of two chapters. The first explores the use of language in Muhammad Yunus's Nobel Peace Prize acceptance speech (2006) and Steve Jobs's Stanford commencement speech (2005). The focus here is on how the abstract system of values defining an ideology shapes the language we use and how language shapes the way we think and our thought. Theoretical background takes into account Lakoff's theory of the metaphorical thought system (1980) which underlies every social and political expression as well as morality itself (1995, 2008). Therefore, a brief introductive paragraph will deal with Lakoff's account, selecting those principles which are relevant to our analysis, paying particular attention to the "narratives".

The second chapter analyses a particular sub-genre of political discourse – the declaration of war – focusing on two addresses to their nation by western leaders – King George VI (1939) and US President Franklin D. Roosevelt (1941) – through which citizens are informed about the new conflict. Following Van Dijk's account on political-critical discourse analysis (1995, 1997), this second chapter aims at highlighting the structures and strategies of the speeches which involve topics, textual schemata, local semantics, lexicon, syntax, and rhetoric. Finally, Lakoff's insight into cognitive metaphors and moral accounting schemes will be taken into consideration as regards the justification of war and its moral implications (1995). Structures and strategies of the speeches are explored in order to show how these are defined by and contribute to reinforcing the "ideological square" and the "political cognition" of the nation.

In general, in order to highlight the underlying ideologies, rhetorical apparatus, lexical choice, syntactic structures, grammar, pronouns distribution, discourse architecture and so on will be identified and commented. Selected principles of linguistics and pragmatics will also guide the analyses since linguistic manipulation and persuasion are based not only on what is said, but especially on what can be *done* with words. In other words, this represents an attempt to conduct a language-based analysis which takes into account why, in ideological terms, secific linguistic choices are made.

The target level of English language required for approaching this book profitably is B2. This level is defined according to the Common European Framework of Reference for Languages (CEFR). On global scale, B2 learner's proficiency level is described as follows.

Can understand the main ideas of complex texts on both concrete and abstract topics, including technical discussions in his/her field of specialisation. Can interact with a degree of fluency and spontaneity that makes regular interaction with native speakers quite possible without strain for either party. Can produce clear, detailed text on a wide range of subjects and explain a viewpoint on a topical issue giving the advantages and disadvantages of various options.

Nevertheless, the book is also suitable for advanced learners interested in going deeper into the matter of English political discourse analysis. This text is firstly and formerly conceived and written as a course book, but it also lends itself for individual study. In this latter case, a better comprehension could be improved by consulting the references listed at the end of each chapter, along with a good dictionary of linguistics.

The transcripts of the speeches and a brief glossary of rhetorical terms are included as appendices, so that following the analyses is made easier.

Chapter 1:
SPEECH TRANSCRIPTS OF:
M.Yunus, S.Jobs, King George VI, Roosevelt

Muhammad Yunus's Nobel Lecture. December 10, 2006, Oslo.

Your Majesties, Your Royal Highnesses, Honourable Members of the Norwegian Nobel Committee, Excellencies, Ladies and Gentlemen, Grameen Bank and I are deeply honoured to receive this most prestigious of awards. We are thrilled and overwhelmed by this honour. Since the Nobel Peace Prize was announced, I have received endless messages from around the world, but what moves me most are the calls I get almost daily, from the borrowers of Grameen Bank in remote Bangladeshi villages, who just want to say how proud they are to have received this recognition.

Nine elected representatives of the 7 million borrowers-cum-owners of Grameen Bank have accompanied me all the way to Oslo to receive the prize. I express thanks on their behalf to the Norwegian Nobel Committee for choosing Grameen Bank for this year's Nobel Peace Prize. By giving their institution the most prestigious prize in the world, you give them unparalleled honour. Thanks to your prize, nine proud women from the villages of Bangladesh are at the ceremony today as Nobel laureates, giving an altogether new meaning to the Nobel Peace Prize.

All borrowers of Grameen Bank are celebrating this day as the greatest day of their lives. They are gathering around the nearest television set in their villages all over Bangladesh , along with other villagers, to watch the proceedings of this ceremony.

This years' prize gives highest honour and dignity to the hundreds of millions of women all around the world who struggle every day to make a living and bring hope for a better life for their children. This is a historic moment for them.

By giving us this prize, the Norwegian Nobel Committee has given important support to the proposition that peace is inextricably linked to poverty. Poverty is a threat to peace.

World's income distribution gives a very telling story. Ninety four percent of the world income goes to 40 percent of the population while sixty percent of people live on only 6 per cent of world income. Half of the world population lives on two dollars a day. Over one billion people live on less than a dollar a day. This is no formula for peace.

The new millennium began with a great global dream. World leaders gathered at the United Nations in 2000 and adopted, among others, a historic goal to reduce poverty by half by 2015. Never in human history had such a bold goal been adopted by the entire world in one voice, one that specified time and size. But then came September 11 and the Iraq war, and suddenly the world became derailed from the pursuit of this dream, with the attention of world leaders shifting from the war on poverty to the war on terrorism. Till now over $ 530 billion has been spent on the war in Iraq by the USA alone.

I believe terrorism cannot be won over by military action. Terrorism must be condemned in the strongest language. We must stand solidly against it, and find all the means to end it. We must address the root causes of terrorism to end it for all time to come. I believe that putting resources into improving the lives of the poor people is a better strategy than spending it on guns.

Peace should be understood in a human way – in a broad social, political and economic way. Peace is threatened by unjust economic, social and political order, absence of democracy, environmental degradation and absence of human rights.

Poverty is the absence of all human rights. The frustrations, hostility and anger generated by abject poverty cannot sustain peace in any society. For building stable peace we must find ways to provide opportunities for people to live decent lives.

The creation of opportunities for the majority of people – the poor – is at the heart of the work that we have dedicated ourselves to during the past 30 years.

I became involved in the poverty issue not as a policymaker or a researcher. I became involved because poverty was all around me, and I could not turn away from it. In 1974, I found it difficult to teach elegant theories of economics in the university classroom, in the backdrop of a terrible famine in Bangladesh. Suddenly, I felt the emptiness of those theories in the face of crushing hunger and poverty. I wanted to do something immediate to help people around me, even if it was just one human being, to get through another day with a little more ease. That brought me face to face with poor people's struggle to find the tiniest amounts of money to support their efforts to eke out a living. I was shocked to discover a woman in the village, borrowing less than a dollar from the money-lender, on the condition that he would have the exclusive right to buy all she produces at the price he decides. This, to me, was a way of recruiting slave labour.

I decided to make a list of the victims of this money-lending "business" in the village next door to our campus.

When my list was done, it had the names of 42 victims who borrowed a total amount of US $27. I offered US $27 from my own pocket to get these victims out of the clutches of those money-lenders. The excitement that was created among the people by this small action got me further involved in it. If I could make so many people so happy with such a tiny amount of money, why not do more of it?

That is what I have been trying to do ever since. The first thing I did was to try to persuade the bank located in the campus to lend money to the poor. But that did not work. The bank said that the poor were not creditworthy. After all my efforts, over several months, failed I offered to become a guarantor for the loans to the poor. I was stunned by the result. The poor paid back their loans, on time, every time! But still I kept confronting difficulties in expanding the program through the existing banks. That was when I decided to create a separate bank for the poor, and in 1983, I finally succeeded in doing that. I named it Grameen Bank or Village bank.

Today, Grameen Bank gives loans to nearly 7.0 million poor people, 97 per cent of whom are women, in 73,000 villages in Bangladesh. Grameen Bank gives collateral-free income generating housing loans, student and micro-enterprise loans to the poor families and offers a host of attractive savings, pension funds and insurance products for its members. Since it introduced them in 1984, housing loans have been used to construct 640,000 houses. The legal ownership of these houses belongs to the women themselves. We focused on women because we found giving loans to women always brought more benefits to the family.

In a cumulative way the bank has given out loans totalling about US $6.0 billion. The repayment rate is 99%. Grameen Bank routinely makes profit. Financially, it is self-reliant and has not taken donor money since 1995. Deposits and own resources of Grameen Bank today amount to 143 per cent of all outstanding loans. According to Grameen Bank's internal survey, 58 per cent of our borrowers have crossed the poverty line.

Grameen Bank was born as a tiny home-grown project run with the help of several of my students, all local girls and boys. Three of these students are still with me in Grameen Bank, after all these years, as its topmost executives. They are here today to receive this honour you give us.

This idea, which began in Jobra, a small village in Bangladesh, has spread around the world and there are now Grameen type programs in almost every country in the world.

It is 30 years now since we began. We keep looking at the children of our borrowers to see what has been the impact of our work on their lives. The women who are our borrowers always gave topmost priority to the children. One of the Sixteen Decisions developed and followed by them was to send children to school. Grameen Bank encouraged them, and before long all the children were going to school. Many of these children made it to the top of their class. We wanted to celebrate that, so we introduced scholarships for talented students. Grameen Bank now gives 30,000 scholarships every year.

Many of the children went on to higher education to become doctors, engineers, college teachers and other professionals. We introduced student loans to make it easy for Grameen students to complete higher education. Now some of them have even PhD's. There are 13,000 students on student loans. Over 7,000 students are added to this number annually.

We are creating a completely new generation that will be well equipped to take their families way out of the reach of poverty. We want to make a break in the historical continuation of poverty.

In Bangladesh 80 percent of the poor families have already been reached with microcredit. We are hoping that by 2010, 100 per cent of the poor families will be reached.

Three years ago we started an exclusive programme focusing on the beggars. None of Grameen Bank's rules apply to them. Loans are interest-free; they can pay whatever amount they wish, whenever they wish. We gave them the idea to carry small merchandise such as snacks, toys for the kids or household items for the housewives, when they went from house to house for begging. The idea worked. There are now 85,000 beggars in the program. About 5,000 of them have already stopped begging completely. They are now house-to-house salespersons rather than house-to-house beggars. Typical loan to a beggar is $12.

We encourage and support every conceivable effective intervention to help the poor fight out of poverty. We always advocate microcredit in addition to all other interventions, arguing that microcredit makes those interventions work better.

Information and communication technology (ICT) is quickly changing the world, creating distanceless, borderless world of instantaneous communications. Increasingly, it is becoming less and less costly. I saw an opportunity for the poor people to change their lives if this technology could be brought to them to meet their needs.

As a first step to bring ICT to the poor we created a mobile phone company, Grameen Phone. We gave loans from Grameen Bank to the poor women to buy mobile phones to sell phone services in the villages. We saw the synergy between microcredit and ICT.

The phone business was a success and became a coveted enterprise for Grameen borrowers. Telephone-ladies quickly learned and innovated the ropes of the telephone business, and it has become the quickest way to get out of poverty and to earn social respectability. Today there are nearly 300,000 telephone ladies providing telephone service in all the villages of Bangladesh. Grameen Phone has more than 10 million subscribers, and is the largest mobile phone company in the country. Although the number of telephone-ladies is only a small fraction of the total number of subscribers, they generate 19 per cent of the revenue of the company. Out of the nine board members who are attending this ceremony today 4 are telephone-ladies.

Grameen Phone is a joint-venture company owned by Telenor of Norway and Grameen Telecom of Bangladesh. Telenor owns 62 per cent share of the company, Grameen Telecom owns 38 per cent. Our vision was to ultimately convert this company into a social business by giving majority ownership to the poor women of Grameen Bank. We are working towards that goal. Someday Grameen Phone will become another example of a big enterprise owned by the poor.

Capitalism centres on the free market. It is claimed that the freer the market, the better is the result of capitalism in solving the questions of what, how, and for whom. It is also claimed that the individual search for personal gains brings collective optimal result.

I am in favour of strengthening the freedom of the market. At the same time, I am very unhappy about the conceptual restrictions imposed on the players in the market. This originates from the assumption that entrepreneurs are one-dimensional human beings, who are dedicated to one mission in their business lives – to maximize profit. This interpretation of capitalism insulates the entrepreneurs from all political, emotional, social, spiritual, environmental dimensions of their lives. This was done perhaps as a reasonable simplification, but it stripped away the very essentials of human life.

Human beings are a wonderful creation embodied with limitless human qualities and capabilities. Our theoretical constructs should make room for the blossoming of those qualities, not assume them away.

Many of the world's problems exist because of this restriction on the players of free-market. The world has not resolved the problem of crushing poverty that half of its population suffers. Healthcare remains out of the reach of the majority of the world population.

We have remained so impressed by the success of the free-market that we never dared to express any doubt about our basic assumption. To make it worse, we worked extra hard to transform ourselves, as closely as possible, into the one-dimensional human beings as conceptualized in the theory, to allow smooth functioning of free market mechanism.

By defining "entrepreneur" in a broader way we can change the character of capitalism radically, and solve many of the unresolved social and economic problems within the scope of the free market. Let us suppose an entrepreneur, instead of having a single source of motivation (such as, maximizing profit), now has two sources of motivation, which are mutually exclusive, but equally compelling – a) maximization of profit and b) doing good to people and the world.

Each type of motivation will lead to a separate kind of business. Let us call the first type of business a profit-maximizing business, and the second type of business as social business.

Social business will be a new kind of business introduced in the market place with the objective of making a difference in the world. Investors in the social business could get back their investment, but will not take any dividend from the company. Profit would be ploughed back into the company to expand its outreach and improve the quality of its product or service. A social business will be a non-loss, non-dividend company.

Once social business is recognized in law, many existing companies will come forward to create social businesses in addition to their foundation activities. Many activists from the non-profit sector will also find this an attractive option. Unlike the non-profit sector where one needs to collect donations to keep activities going, a social business will be self-sustaining and create surplus for expansion since it is a non-loss enterprise. Social business will go into a new type of capital market of its own, to raise capital.

Young people all around the world, particularly in rich countries, will find the concept of social business very appealing since it will give them a challenge to make a difference by using their creative talent. Many young people today feel frustrated because they cannot see any worthy challenge, which excites them, within the present capitalist world. Socialism gave them a dream to fight for. Young people dream about creating a perfect world of their own.

Almost all social and economic problems of the world will be addressed through social businesses. The challenge is to innovate business models and apply them to produce desired social results cost-effectively and efficiently. Healthcare for the poor, financial services for the poor, information technology for the poor, education and training for the poor, marketing for the poor, renewable energy – these are all exciting areas for social businesses.

Social business is important because it addresses very vital concerns of mankind. It can change the lives of the bottom 60 per cent of world population and help them to get out of poverty.

Even profit maximizing companies can be designed as social businesses by giving full or majority ownership to the poor. This constitutes a second type of social business. Grameen Bank falls under this category of social business. It is owned by the poor.

The poor could get the shares of these companies as gifts by donors, or they could buy the shares with their own money. The borrowers with their own money buy Grameen Bank shares, which cannot be transferred to non-borrowers. A committed professional team does the day-to-day running of the bank.

Bilateral and multi-lateral donors could easily create this type of social business. When a donor gives a loan or a grant to build a bridge in the recipient country, it could create a "bridge company" owned by the local poor. A committed management company could be given the responsibility of running the company. Profit of the company will go to the local poor as dividend, and towards building more bridges. Many infrastructure projects, like roads, highways, airports, seaports, utility companies could all be built in this manner.

Grameen has created two social businesses of the first type. One is a yogurt factory, to produce fortified yogurt to bring nutrition to malnourished children, in a joint venture with Danone. It will continue to expand until all malnourished children of Bangladesh are reached with this yogurt. Another is a chain of eye-care hospitals. Each hospital will undertake 10,000 cataract surgeries per year at differentiated prices to the rich and the poor.

To connect investors with social businesses, we need to create social stock market where only the shares of social businesses will be traded. An investor will come to this stock-exchange with a clear intention of finding a social business, which has a mission of his liking. Anyone who wants to make money will go to the existing stock-market.

To enable a social stock-exchange to perform properly, we will need to create rating agencies, standardization of terminology, definitions, impact measurement tools, reporting formats, and new financial publications, such as, The Social Wall Street Journal. Business schools will offer courses and business management degrees on social businesses to train young managers how to manage social business enterprises in the most efficient manner, and, most of all, to inspire them to become social business entrepreneurs themselves.

I support globalization and believe it can bring more benefits to the poor than its alternative. But it must be the right kind of globalization. To me, globalization is like a hundred-lane highway criss-crossing the world. If it is a free-for-all highway, its lanes will be taken over by the giant trucks from powerful economies. Bangladeshi rickshaw will be thrown off the highway. In order to have a win-win globalization we must have traffic rules, traffic police, and traffic authority for this global highway. Rule of "strongest takes it all" must be replaced by rules that ensure that the poorest have a place and piece of the action, without being elbowed out by the strong. Globalization must not become financial imperialism.

Powerful multi-national social businesses can be created to retain the benefit of globalization for the poor people and poor countries. Social businesses will either bring ownership to the poor people, or keep the profit within the poor countries, since taking dividends will not be their objective. Direct foreign investment by foreign social businesses will be exciting news for recipient countries. Building strong economies in the poor countries by protecting their national interest from plundering companies will be a major area of interest for the social businesses.

We get what we want, or what we don't refuse. We accept the fact that we will always have poor people around us, and that poverty is part of human destiny. This is precisely why we continue to have poor people around us. If we firmly believe that poverty is unacceptable to us, and that it should not belong to a civilized society, we would have built appropriate institutions and policies to create a poverty-free world.

We wanted to go to the moon, so we went there. We achieve what we want to achieve. If we are not achieving something, it is because we have not put our minds to it. We create what we want.

What we want and how we get to it depends on our mindsets. It is extremely difficult to change mindsets once they are formed. We create the world in accordance with our mindset. We need to invent ways to change our perspective continually and reconfigure our mindset quickly as new knowledge emerges. We can reconfigure our world if we can reconfigure our mindset.

I believe that we can create a poverty-free world because poverty is not created by poor people. It has been created and sustained by the economic and social system that we have designed for ourselves; the institutions and concepts that make up that system; the policies that we pursue.

Poverty is created because we built our theoretical framework on assumptions which under-estimates human capacity, by designing concepts, which are too narrow (such as concept of business, credit- worthiness, entrepreneurship, employment) or developing institutions, which remain half-done (such as financial institutions, where poor are left out). Poverty is caused by the failure at the conceptual level, rather than any lack of capability on the part of people.

I firmly believe that we can create a poverty-free world if we collectively believe in it. In a poverty-free world, the only place you would be able to see poverty is in the poverty museums. When school children take a tour of the poverty museums, they would be horrified to see the misery and indignity that some human beings had to go through. They would blame their forefathers for tolerating this inhuman condition, which existed for so long, for so many people.

A human being is born into this world fully equipped not only to take care of him or herself, but also to contribute to enlarging the well being of the world as a whole. Some get the chance to explore their potential to some degree, but many others never get any opportunity, during their lifetime, to unwrap the wonderful gift they were born with. They die unexplored and the world remains deprived of their creativity, and their contribution.

Grameen has given me an unshakeable faith in the creativity of human beings. This has led me to believe that human beings are not born to suffer the misery of hunger and poverty.

To me poor people are like bonsai trees. When you plant the best seed of the tallest tree in a flower-pot, you get a replica of the tallest tree, only inches tall. There is nothing wrong with the seed you planted, only the soil-base that is too inadequate. Poor people are bonsai people. There is nothing wrong in their seeds. Simply, society never gave them the base to grow on. All it needs to get the poor people out of poverty for us to create an enabling environment for them. Once the poor can unleash their energy and creativity, poverty will disappear very quickly.

Let us join hands to give every human being a fair chance to unleash their energy and creativity.

Ladies and Gentlemen,

Let me conclude by expressing my deep gratitude to the Norwegian Nobel Committee for recognizing that poor people, and especially poor women, have both the potential and the right to live a decent life, and that microcredit helps to unleash that potential.

I believe this honour that you give us will inspire many more bold initiatives around the world to make a historical breakthrough in ending global poverty.

Thank you very much.

Steve Jobs's Commencement Address. June 12, 2005, Stanford University.

I am honored to be with you today at your commencement from one of the finest universities in the world. Truth be told, I never graduated from college and this is the closest I've ever gotten to a college graduation. Today I want to tell you three stories from my life. That's it. No big deal. Just three stories.

The first story is about connecting the dots.

I dropped out of Reed College after the first 6 months, but then stayed around as a drop-in for another 18 months or so before I really quit. So why did I drop out?

It started before I was born. My biological mother was a young, unwed college graduate student, and she decided to put me up for adoption. She felt very strongly that I should be adopted by college graduates, so everything was all set for me to be adopted at birth by a lawyer and his wife. Except that when I popped out they decided at the last minute that they really wanted a girl. So my parents, who were on a waiting list, got a call in the middle of the night asking: "We have an unexpected baby boy; do you want him?" They said: "Of course." My biological mother found out later that my mother had never graduated from college and that my father had never graduated from high school. She refused to sign the final adoption papers. She only relented a few months later when my parents promised that I would someday go to college. This was the start in my life.

And 17 years later I did go to college. But I naively chose a college that was almost as expensive as Stanford, and all of my working-class parents' savings were being spent on my college tuition. After six months, I couldn't see the value in it. I had no idea what I wanted to do with my life and no idea how college was going to help me figure it out. And here I was spending all of the money my parents had saved their entire life. So I decided to drop out and trust that it would all work out OK. It was pretty scary at the time, but looking back it was one of the best decisions I ever made. The minute I dropped out I could stop taking the required classes that didn't interest me, and begin dropping in on the ones that looked far more interesting.

It wasn't all romantic. I didn't have a dorm room, so I slept on the floor in friends' rooms, I returned coke bottles for the 5¢ deposits to buy food with, and I would walk the 7 miles across town every Sunday night to get one good meal a week at the Hare Krishna temple. I loved it. And much of what I stumbled into by following my curiosity and intuition turned out to be priceless later on. Let me give you one example:

Reed College at that time offered perhaps the best calligraphy instruction in the country. Throughout the campus every poster, every label on every drawer, was beautifully hand calligraphed. Because I had dropped out and didn't have to take the normal classes, I decided to take a calligraphy class to learn how to do this. I learned about serif and san serif typefaces, about varying the amount of space between different letter combinations, about what makes great typography great. It was beautiful, historical, artistically subtle in a way that science can't capture, and I found it fascinating.

None of this had even a hope of any practical application in my life. But ten years later, when we were designing the first Macintosh computer, it all came back to me. And we designed it all into the Mac. It was the first computer with beautiful typography. If I had never dropped in on that single course in college, the Mac would have never had multiple typefaces or proportionally spaced fonts. And since Windows just copied the Mac, it's likely that no personal computer would have them. If I had never dropped out, I would have never dropped in on this calligraphy class, and personal computers might not have the wonderful typography that they do. Of course it was impossible to connect the dots looking forward when I was in college. But it was very, very clear looking backwards ten years later.

Again, you can't connect the dots looking forward; you can only connect them looking backwards. So you have to trust that the dots will somehow connect in your future. You have to trust in something — your gut, destiny, life, karma, whatever. Because believe in the dots connect down the road will give you the confidence to follow your heart even when it leads you off the well-worn path and that would make all the difference.

My second story is about love and loss.

I was lucky — I found what I loved to do early in life. Woz and I started Apple in my parents garage when I was 20. We worked hard, and in 10 years Apple had grown from just the two of us in a garage into a $2 billion company with over 4000 employees. We had just released our finest creation — the Macintosh — a year earlier, and I had just turned 30. And then I got fired. How can you get fired from a company you started? Well, as Apple grew we hired someone who I thought was very talented to run the company with me, and for the first year or so things went well. But then our visions of the future began to diverge and eventually we had a falling out. When we did, our Board of Directors sided with him. So at 30 I was out. And very publicly out. What had been the focus of my entire adult life was gone, and it was devastating.

I really didn't know what to do for a few months. I felt that I had let the previous generation of entrepreneurs down - that I had dropped the baton as it was being passed to me. I met with David Packard and Bob Noyce and tried to apologize for screwing up so badly. I was a very public failure, and I even thought about running away from the valley. But something slowly began to dawn on me — I still loved what I did. The turn of events at Apple had not changed that one bit. I had been rejected, but I was still in love. And so I decided to start over.

I didn't see it then, but it turned out that getting fired from Apple was the best thing that could have ever happened to me. The heaviness of being successful was replaced by the lightness of being a beginner again, less sure about everything. It freed me to enter one of the most creative periods of my life.

During the next five years, I started a company named NeXT, another company named Pixar, and fell in love with an amazing woman who would become my wife. Pixar went on to create the worlds first computer animated feature film, *Toy Story*, and is now the most successful animation studio in the world. In a remarkable turn of events, Apple bought NeXT, I returned to Apple, and the technology we developed at NeXT is at the heart of Apple's current renaissance. And Laurene and I have a wonderful family together.

I'm pretty sure none of this would have happened if I hadn't been fired from Apple. It was awful tasting medicine, but I guess the patient needed it. Sometimes life hits you in the head with a brick. Don't lose faith. I'm convinced that the only thing that kept me going was that I loved what I did. You've got to find what you love. And that is as true for your work as it is for your lovers. Your work is going to fill a large part of your life, and the only way to be truly satisfied is to do what you believe is great work. And the only way to do great work is to love what you do. If you haven't found it yet, keep looking. Don't settle. As with all matters of the heart, you'll know when you find it. And, like any great relationship, it just gets better and better as the years roll on. So keep looking until you find it. Don't settle.

My third story is about death.

When I was 17, I read a quote that went something like: "If you live each day as if it was your last, someday you'll most certainly be right." It made an impression on me, and since then, for the past 33 years, I have looked in the mirror every morning and asked myself: "If today were the last day of my life, would I want to do what I am about to do today?" And whenever the answer has been "No" for too many days in a row, I know I need to change something.

Remembering that I'll be dead soon is the most important tool I've ever encountered to help me make the big choices in life. Because almost everything — all external expectations, all pride, all fear of embarrassment or failure - these things just fall away in the face of death, leaving only what is truly important. Remembering that you are going to die is the best way I know to avoid the trap of thinking you have something to lose. You are already naked. There is no reason not to follow your heart.

About a year ago I was diagnosed with cancer. I had a scan at 7:30 in the morning, and it clearly showed a tumor on my pancreas. I didn't even know what a pancreas was. The doctors told me this was almost certainly a type of cancer that is incurable, and that I should expect to live no longer than three to six months. My doctor advised me to go home and get my affairs in order, which is doctor's code for prepare to die. It means to try to tell your kids everything you thought you'd have the next 10 years to tell them in just a few months. It means to make sure everything is buttoned up so that it will be as easy as possible for your family. It means to say your goodbyes.

I lived with that diagnosis all day. Later that evening I had a biopsy, where they stuck an endoscope down my throat, through my stomach and into my intestines, put a needle into my pancreas and got a few cells from the tumor. I was sedated, but my wife, who was there, told me that when they viewed the cells under a microscope the doctors started crying because it turned out to be a very rare form of pancreatic cancer that is curable with surgery. I had the surgery and thankfully I'm fine now.

This was the closest I've been to facing death, and I hope it's the closest I get for a few more decades. Having lived through it, I can now say this to you with a bit more certainty than when death was a useful but purely intellectual concept:

No one wants to die. Even people who want to go to heaven don't want to die to get there. And yet death is the destination we all share. No one has ever escaped it. And that is as it should be, because Death is very likely the single best invention of Life. It is Life's change agent. It clears out the old to make way for the new. Right now the new is you, but someday not too long from now, you will gradually become the old and be cleared away. Sorry to be so dramatic, but it is quite true.

Your time is limited, so don't waste it living someone else's life. Don't be trapped by dogma — which is living with the results of other people's thinking. Don't let the noise of others' opinions drown out your own inner voice. And most important, have the courage to follow your heart and intuition. They somehow already know what you truly want to become. Everything else is secondary.

When I was young, there was an amazing publication called *The Whole Earth Catalog*, which was one of the bibles of my generation. It was created by a fellow named Stewart Brand not far from here in Menlo Park, and he brought it to life with his poetic touch. This was in the late 1960's, before personal computers and desktop publishing, so it was all made with typewriters, scissors, and polaroid cameras. It was sort of like Google in paperback form, 35 years before Google came along: it was idealistic, and overflowing with neat tools and great notions.

Stewart and his team put out several issues of *The Whole Earth Catalog*, and then when it had run its course, they put out a final issue. It was the mid-1970s, and I was your age. On the back cover of their final issue was a photograph of an early morning country road, the kind you might find yourself hitchhiking on if you were so adventurous. Beneath it were the words: "Stay Hungry. Stay Foolish." It was their farewell message as they signed off. Stay Hungry. Stay Foolish. And I have always wished that for myself. And now, as you graduate to begin anew, I wish that for you.

Stay Hungry. Stay Foolish.

Thank you all very much.

George VI, Broadcast, outbreak of war with Germany. September 3, 1939.

In this grave hour, perhaps the most fateful in our history, I send to every household of my peoples, both at home and overseas, this message, spoken with the same depth of feeling for each one of you as if I were able to cross your threshold and speak to you myself.

For the second time in the lives of most of us we are at war. Over and over again we have tried to find a peaceful way out of the differences between ourselves and those who are now our enemies. But it has been in vain. We have been forced into a conflict. For we are called, with our allies, to meet the challenge of a principle which, if it were to prevail, would be fatal to any civilised order in the world.

It is the principle which permits a state, in the selfish pursuit of power, to disregard its treaties and its solemn pledges; which sanctions the use of force, or threat of force, against the sovereignty and independence of other states. Such a principle, stripped of all disguise, is surely the mere primitive doctrine that might is right; and if this principle were established throughout the world, the freedom of our own country and of the whole British Commonwealth of Nations would be in danger. But far more than this - the peoples of the world would be kept in the bondage of fear, and all hopes of settled peace and of the security of justice and liberty among nations would be ended.

This is the ultimate issue which confronts us. For the sake of all that we ourselves hold dear, and of the world's order and peace, it is unthinkable that we should refuse to meet the challenge.

It is to this high purpose that I now call my people at home and my peoples across the seas, who will make our cause their own. I ask them to stand calm, firm, and united in this time of trial. The task will be hard. There may be dark days ahead, and war can no longer be confined to the battlefield. But we can only do the right as we see the right, and reverently commit our cause to God. If one and all we keep resolutely faithful to it, ready for whatever service or sacrifice it may demand, then, with God's help, we shall prevail.

May He bless and keep us all.

Franklin Delano Roosevelt, 19th Fireside chat (broadcast). December 9, 1941.

My fellow citizens,

The sudden criminal attacks perpetrated by the Japanese in the Pacific provide the climax of a decade of international immorality.

Powerful and resourceful gangsters have banded together to make war upon the whole human race. Their challenge has now been flung at the United States of America. The Japanese have treacherously violated the long-standing peace between us. Many American soldiers and sailors have been killed by enemy action. American ships have been sunk; American airplanes have been destroyed.

The Congress and the people of the United States have accepted that challenge.

Together with other free peoples, we are now fighting to maintain our right to live among our world neighbors in freedom and in common decency, without fear of assault.

I have prepared the full record of our past relations with Japan, and it will be submitted to the Congress. It begins with the visit of Commodore Perry to Japan 88 years ago. It ends with the visit of two Japanese emissaries to the Secretary of State last Sunday, an hour after Japanese forces had loosed their bombs and machine guns against our flag, our forces, and our citizens.

I can say with utmost confidence that no Americans, today or a thousand years hence, need feel anything but pride in our patience and in our efforts through all the years toward achieving a peace in the Pacific which would be fair and honorable to every Nation, large or small. And no honest person, today or a thousand years hence, will be able to suppress a sense of indignation and horror at the treachery committed by the military dictators of Japan, under the very shadow of the flag of peace borne by their special envoys in our midst.

The course that Japan has followed for the past ten years in Asia has paralleled the course of Hitler and Mussolini in Europe and in Africa. Today, it has become far more than a parallel. It is actual collaboration so well calculated that all the continents of the world, and all the oceans, are now considered by the Axis strategists as one gigantic battlefield.

In 1931, ten years ago, Japan invaded Manchukuo—without warning.

In 1935, Italy invaded Ethiopia—without warning.

In 1938, Hitler occupied Austria —without warning.

In 1939, Hitler invaded Czechoslovakia- without warning.

Later in 1939, Hitler invaded Poland- without warning.

In 1940, Hitler invaded Norway, Denmark, the Netherlands, Belgium, and Luxembourg- without warning.

In 1940, Italy attacked France and later Greece—without warning.

And this year, in 1941, the Axis powers attacked Yugoslavia and Greece and they dominated the Balkans—without warning. In 1941, also, Hitler invaded Russia—without warning.

And now Japan has attacked Malaya and Thailand—and the United States —without warning.

It is all of one pattern.

We are now in this war. We are all in it- all the way. Every single man, woman, and child is a partner in the most tremendous undertaking of our American history. We must share together the bad news and the good news, the defeats and the victories—the changing fortunes of war.

So far, the news has been all bad. We have suffered a serious set-back in Hawaii. Our forces in the Philippines, which include the brave people of that Commonwealth, are taking punishment, but are defending themselves vigorously. The reports from Guam and Wake and Midway islands are still confused, but we must be prepared for the announcement that all these three outposts have been seized.

The casualty lists of these first few days will undoubtedly be large. I deeply feel the anxiety of all of the families of the men in our armed forces and the relatives of people in cities which have been bombed. I can only give them my solemn promise that they will get news just as quickly as possible.

This Government will put its trust in the stamina of the American people, and will give the facts to the public just as soon as two conditions have been fulfilled: first, that the information has been definitely and officially confirmed; and, second, that the release of the information at the time it is received will not prove valuable to the enemy directly or indirectly.

Most earnestly I urge my countrymen to reject all rumors. These ugly little hints of complete disaster fly thick and fast in wartime. They have to be examined and appraised.

As an example, I can tell you frankly that until further surveys are made, I have not sufficient information to state the exact damage which has been done to our naval vessels at Pearl Harbor. Admittedly the damage is serious. But no one can say how serious, until we know how much of this damage can be repaired and how quickly the necessary repairs can be made.

I cite as another example a statement made on Sunday night that a Japanese carrier had been located and sunk off the Canal Zone. And when you hear statements that are attributed to what they call "an authoritative source," you can be reasonably sure from now on that under these war circumstances the "authoritative source" is not any person in authority.

Many rumors and reports which we now hear originate with enemy sources. For instance, today the Japanese are claiming that as a result of their one action against Hawaii they have gained naval supremacy in the Pacific. This is an old trick of propaganda which has been used innumerable times by the Nazis. The purposes of such fantastic claims are, of course, to spread fear and confusion among us, and to goad us into revealing military information which our enemies are desperately anxious to obtain.

Our Government will not be caught in this obvious trap—and neither will the people of the United States.

It must be remembered by each and every one of us that our free and rapid communication these days must be greatly restricted in wartime. It is not possible to receive full, speedy, accurate reports from distant areas of combat. This is particularly true where naval operations are concerned. For in these days of the marvels of radio it is often impossible for the commanders of various units to report their activities by radio at all, for the very simple reason that this information would become available to the enemy, and would disclose their position and their plan of defense or attack.

Of necessity there will be delays in officially confirming or denying reports of operations but we will not hide facts from the country if we know the facts and if the enemy will not be aided by their disclosure.

To all newspapers and radio stations—all those who reach the eyes and ears of the American people—I say this: You have a most grave responsibility to the Nation now and for the duration of this war.

If you feel that your Government is not disclosing enough of the truth, you have every right to say so. But—in the absence of all the facts, as revealed by official sources—you have no right in the ethics of patriotism to deal out unconfirmed reports in such a way as to make people believe that they are gospel truth.

Every citizen, in every walk of life,. shares this same responsibility. The lives of our soldiers and sailors- the whole future of this Nation—depend upon the manner in which each and every one of us fulfills his obligation to our country.

Now a word about the recent past—and the future. A year and a half has elapsed since the fall of France, when the whole world first realized the mechanized might which the Axis Nations had been building for so many years. America has used that year and a half to great advantage. Knowing that the attack might reach us in all too short a time, we immediately began greatly to increase our industrial strength and our capacity to meet the demands of modern warfare.

Precious months were gained by sending vast quantities of our war material to the Nations of the world still able to resist Axis aggression. Our policy rested on the fundamental truth that the defense of any country resisting Hitler or Japan was in the long run the defense of our own country. That policy has been justified. It has given us time, invaluable time, to build our American assembly lines of production.

Assembly lines are now in operation. Others are being rushed to completion. A steady stream of tanks and planes, of guns and ships, and shells and equipment—that is what these eighteen months have given us.

But it is all only a beginning of what still has to be done. We must be set to face a long war against crafty and powerful bandits. The attack at Pearl Harbor can be repeated at any one of many points, points in both oceans and along both our coast lines and against all the rest of the hemisphere.

It will not only be a long war, it will be a hard war. That is the basis on which we now lay all our plans. That is the yardstick by which we measure what we shall need and demand; money, materials, doubled and quadrupled production—ever-increasing. The production must be not only for our own Army and Navy and Air Forces. It must reinforce the other armies and navies and air forces fighting the Nazis and the war lords of Japan throughout the Americas and throughout the world.

I have been working today on the subject of production. Your Government has decided on two broad policies.

The first is to speed up all existing production by working on a seven-day-week basis in every war industry, including the production of essential raw materials.

The second policy, now being put into form, is to rush additions to the capacity of production by building more new plants, by adding to old plants, and by using the many smaller plants for war needs.

Over the hard road of the past months, we have at times met obstacles and difficulties, divisions and disputes, indifference and callousness. That is now all past—and, I am sure, forgotten.

The fact is that the country now has an organization in Washington built around men and women who are recognized experts in their own fields. I think the country knows that the people who are actually responsible in each and every one of these many fields are pulling together with a teamwork that has never before been excelled.

On the road ahead there lies hard work—grueling workday and night, every hour and every minute.

I was about to add that ahead there lies sacrifice for all of us.

But it is not correct to use that word. The United States does not consider it a sacrifice to do all one can, to give one's best to our Nation, when the Nation is fighting for its existence and its future life.

It is not a sacrifice for any man, old or young, to be in the Army or the Navy of the United States. Rather is it a privilege.

It is not a sacrifice for the industrialist or the wage earner, the farmer or the shopkeeper, the trainman or the doctor, to pay more taxes, to buy more bonds, to forego extra profits, to work longer or harder at the task for which he is best fitted. Rather is it a privilege.

It is not a sacrifice to do without many things to which we are accustomed if the national defense calls for doing without.

A review this morning leads me to the conclusion that at present we shall not have to curtail the normal use of articles of food. There is enough food today for all of us and enough left over to send to those who are fighting on the same side with us.

But there will be a clear and definite shortage of metals of many kinds for civilian use, for the very good reason that in our increased program we shall need for war purposes more than half of that portion of the principal metals which during the past year have gone into articles for civilian use. Yes, we shall have to give up many things entirely.

And I am sure that the people in every part of the Nation are prepared in their individual living to win this war. I am sure that they will cheerfully help to pay a large part of its financial cost while it goes on. I am sure they will cheerfully give up those material things that they are asked to give up.

And I am sure that they will retain all those great spiritual things without which we cannot win through.

I repeat that the United States can accept no result save victory, final and complete. Not only must the shame of Japanese treachery be wiped out, but the sources of international brutality, wherever they exist, must be absolutely and finally broken.

In my message to the Congress yesterday I said that we "will make it very certain that this form of treachery shall never again endanger us." In order to achieve that certainty, we must begin the great task that is before us by abandoning once and for all the illusion that we can ever again isolate ourselves from the rest of humanity.

In these past few years- and, most violently, in the past three days- we have learned a terrible lesson.

It is our obligation to our dead—it is our sacred obligation' to their children and to our children-that we must never forget what we have learned.

And what we all have learned is this:

There is no such thing as security for any Nation—or any individual- in a world ruled by the principles of gangsterism.

There is no such thing as impregnable defense against powerful aggressors who sneak up in the dark and strike without warning.

We have learned that our ocean-girt hemisphere is not immune from severe attack—that we cannot measure our safety in terms of miles on any map any more.

We may acknowledge that our enemies have performed a brilliant feat of deception, perfectly timed and executed with great skill. It was a thoroughly dishonorable deed, but we must face the fact that modern warfare as conducted in the Nazi manner is a dirty business. We don't like it- we didn't want to get in it -but we are in it and we're going to fight it with everything we've got.

I do not think any American has any doubt of our ability to administer proper punishment to the perpetrators of these crimes.

Your Government knows that for weeks Germany has been telling Japan that if Japan did not attack the United States, Japan would not share in dividing the spoils with Germany when peace came. She was promised by Germany that if she came in she would receive the complete and perpetual control of the whole of the Pacific area—and that means not only the Far East, but also all of the islands in the Pacific, and also a stranglehold on the west coast of North, Central, and South America.

We know also that Germany and Japan are conducting their military and naval operations in accordance with a joint plan. That plan considers all peoples and Nations which are not helping the Axis powers as common enemies of each and every one of the Axis powers.

That is their simple and obvious grand strategy. And that is why the American people must realize that it can be matched only with similar grand strategy. We must realize for example that Japanese successes against the United States in the Pacific are helpful to German operations in Libya; that any German success against the Caucasus is inevitably an assistance to Japan in her operations against the Dutch East Indies; that a German attack against Algiers or Morocco opens the way to a German attack against South America, and the Canal.

On the other side of the picture, we must learn also to know that guerrilla warfare against the Germans in, let us say, Serbia or Norway helps us; that a successful Russian offensive against the Germans helps us; and that British successes on land or sea in any part of the world strengthen our hands.

Remember always that Germany and Italy, regardless of any formal declaration of war, consider themselves at war with the United States at this moment just as much as they consider themselves at war with Britain or Russia. And Germany puts all the other Republics of the Americas into the same category of enemies. The people of our sister Republics of this hemisphere can 'be honored by that fact.

The true goal we seek is far above and beyond the ugly field of battle. When we resort to force, as now we must, we are determined that this force shall be directed toward ultimate good as well as against immediate evil. We Americans are not destroyers —we are builders.

We are now in the midst of a war, not for conquest, not for vengeance, but for a world in which this Nation, and all that this Nation represents, will be safe for our children. We expect to eliminate the danger from Japan, but it would serve us ill if we accomplished that and found that the rest of the world was dominated by Hitler and Mussolini.

We are going to win the war and we are going to win the peace that follows.

And in the difficult hours of this day—through dark days that may be yet to come- we will know that the vast majority of the members of the human race are on our side. Many of them are fighting with us. All of them are praying for us. For in representing our cause, we represent theirs as well- our hope and their hope for liberty under God.

Chapter 2:
STORYTELLING TIME:
M.Yunus's and S.Jobs's Speeches

1.1 Theoretical background, tools of analysis and aims.

This paper aims to explore the use of language in two very famous speeches – Muhammad Yunus's Nobel Peace Prize acceptance speech (2006) and Steve Jobs's Stanford commencement speech (2005) – in order to highlight the underlying ideologies which inform their rhetorical apparatus, lexical choice, syntactic structures, grammar, pronouns distribution, discourse architecture and so on. This represents an attempt to conduct a language-based analysis which takes into account why, in ideological terms, specific linguistic choices are made. Language has a powerful role in establishing, maintaining and also changing ideologies. As Althusser (1971), Pêcheux (1982) Van Dijk (1997), Fairclough (1992) Wodak (1995) and others claim, ideology is a material social fact in language, text and discourse. Ideology here refers to "the system of ideas, beliefs and practises, and representations, which operate in the interests of an identifiable social class or cultural group" (Luke 1998: 366). How this abstract system of values becomes actualized in language and how language contributes to shape it will be explored taking into account Lakoff's theory of the metaphorical thought system (1980) which underlies every social and political expression as well as morality itself (1995, 2008).

These two speeches belong to the same historical period and they were uttered in similar circumstances (i.e. award or degree acceptance ceremonies). Both messages have been highly influential in the worldwide panorama since the two speakers are well-known personalities and their speeches address people virtually all around the world. Yunus's and Jobs's speeches have been chosen since they represent what might be called *telling* narratives: focusing on personal experiences, they not only tell *their* story but foreground a cluster of cross-cultural narratives and schemes. Their stories are proposed as a model of behaviour and ultimately a way of interpreting the world, and their strength lies in being shaped on already existing mental scripts. I have defined them as *telling* narratives because they tell far more than is actually told. People love listening to stories because it is through narratives that our brain conceptualizes and understands reality.

Let us start by examining Lakoff's account and selecting those principles which are relevant to our analysis.

1.2 Ideology and morality beyond (and underneath) words

Most of what we understand in public discourse is not in the words themselves, but in the unconscious understanding that we bring to the words (Lakoff 2008: 43).

Lakoff and Johnson maintain that our understanding of reality is mediated by language and, furthermore, that this is so in a reciprocal sense: language shapes the way we think and our thought shapes the language we use. Concept, mental structure and language are inextricably interwoven. What we see, hear or read is *conceived* through a number of brain structures which in turn are *construed* by language (Kövecses 2010: 8).

Lakoff calls these patterns "frames, metaphors, narratives, image schemas, prototypes, metonymies" (2008: 232) which are both structured by and provided with intellectual/emotional content. No new piece of information we get has a meaning in itself: it is our cognitive system that gives it sense based on *what* we already know and, above all, according to *how* this knowledge is already organized in our mind.

Frames are simple mental paths which we unconsciously follow and think with while formulating an idea, judging or evaluating something or someone. Though they are partially innate, they are rinforced by repeated cultural, physical and emotional experience. It is a matter of neural connection, brain structure and intellectual/emotional content given in a specific cultural context and environment. As a result, in everyday life our most commonplace thoughts follow a set of ready-made networks of links.

The system works by connecting and organizing thoughts in a highly metaphorical way. This means that we *think* in metaphors: we understand one conceptual domain (typically abstract, called TARGET DOMAIN) in terms of another conceptual domain (usually more concrete, defined SOURCE DOMAIN) (Kövecses 2010: 8). Physical experiences in the real world are used as a basis for comprehending more abstract concepts. A classic example of a *conceptual metaphor* is provided by some expressions English speakers often use talking about 'arguments':

The *battle lines* have been drawn between those who accept the changes and those who are against the proposed reforms.

I didn't agree with my colleague's decision, but for the sake of peace, I decided to *bury the hatchet*.

Your claims are *indefensible*.

He *attacked every weak point* in my argument.

I *demolished* his argument.

I've never *won* an argument with him.

You disagree? Okay, *shoot*!

The conceptual metaphor that underlies all these *linguistic* metaphors is ARGUMENT IS WAR. Thinking in metaphor implies not only *speaking* in terms of the source domain, but structuring our actions according to them. In other words it means *living by metaphors* (Lakoff and Johnson 1980).

Frames are gathered in more complex structures to form *narratives*: a typical narrative scheme provides for characters, rules, setting and a time structure (preconditions, build-up, the main event, the purpose, the wind-down, the result and later consequences) (Lakoff 2008: 26). An example of such narratives is the "Rags-to-Riches" pattern: "the initial state of the Protagonist is poverty, where the appropriate emotion is sadness; then there are intermediate states of hard work with varying emotions of frustration and satisfaction; and finally a state of wealth, with the emotions of joy and pride" (Lakoff 2008: 23). Among others one may mention the Troubled Life narrative, the Redemption narrative and the Rescue narrative. Though different cultures will be likely to fill these structures with their own prototypes, themes and images, the basic patterns remain the same as they are *deep narratives*. These structures are unconsciously used for evaluating and interpreting real people (politicians, VIPs, people we know) as well as fictional ones.

The "dark side" of the metaphorical structuring of concepts consists in its being partial in many respects. First, because the source domain will never completely match the target domain, so that metaphors tend to foreground those aspects of the concept which are consistent with the concrete images in use and, at the same time, they prevent us from focusing on other inconsistent concept features by hiding them. Let us consider, for example, the conceptual metaphor LOVE IS WAR. Among other things, it does not take into account the cooperative aspects of love relationships, while it foregrounds the conflicting ones. Secondly, every metaphor in its understanding is context - dependent. Dealing with a metaphor, a number of factors must be allowed for: in which period it is uttered, to whom it is addressed, which aspects of the addressees' cultural and environmental background it refers to, etc. Let us think about Steve Job's advice to Stanford university students: "stay hungry", then try to imagine how starving Bengali people might interpret it.

Lastly, to some extent the metaphorical process as a vehicle for understanding implies the idea that there is an absolute objective truth which is the one embedded in that closed set of culture specific, historically and environmentally determined metaphors largely used in one group of people for interpreting reality. This set can be considered as corresponding to the definition of *ideology*.

It should not be surprising that what concerns our concept of ideology is shaped metaphorically in the brain and in language. According to Luke (1998: 366), ideology refers to "the system of ideas, beliefs and practises, and representations, which operate in the interests of an identifiable social class or cultural group". But this abstract system of values becomes actualized in a metaphorical thought system. Since early childhood everyday experience within our culture and our family contributes to create such an extensive system of metaphors. The correlation between what is physically perceived as pleasant or unpleasant and what is morally good or bad is acquired very early in human life. Abstract concepts, such as morality, are conveyed through our basic physical experiences in a metaphorical representation: since rotten food is not good, immorality will be conceived as rottenness, while purity is associated with morality (Lakoff 2008: 94). The two contrastive concepts, i.e. good and evil, underlie every ideology: if we assume that morality is about right behaviour that leads to well-being – "the well being of oneself, others, and the groups one belongs to: family, community, business, nation" (Lakoff 2008: 93) – we can conclude that ideology is a body of "moral frames", namely a cluster of metaphors which are structured in accordance with accepted standards of morality. The same metaphors for morality are widespread around the world, due to the same ideal well-being conditions which are shared by every culture. Different ideological frameworks are thus informed by the different *priorities* given to the moral metaphors they consist of.

Conceptual metaphors for morality include STRENGTH, HEALTH, PURITY and, above all, WEALTH (receiving good is a gain, being harmed is a loss, and so on). In other words, "moral action is conceptualized in terms of financial transaction" (Lakoff 1995: 178). Hence Lakoff classifies a small number of "moral accounting schemes", that is logics that organize financial transaction of the moral action and which differ according to how the harm (i.e. the debt) is managed. Following the "revenge scheme", for instance, receiving harm ties oneself to taking something of positive value from the offender; if we are in the "altruism scheme", instead, the debts are cancelled, etc. Different ideologies usually refer to different accounting schemes. Moreover, the structure of ideologies (i.e. their hierarchy of values) is organized according to the SOCIETY (or nation) IS A FAMILY conceptual metaphor. But what *kind* of family? In his work *Metaphor, Morality and Politics* (1995), Lakoff compares conservative and liberal ideologies, establishing a strong bond between their issues (world, economic, social, political view) and the family model that underlies them. *Strict father* and *nurturant* father are the referring models, and can be considered universal since they are shared by every culture. They serve as a source domain for understanding society as well as government. In a certain sense family models are comparable to a catalyst, i.e. a metaphorical core that unifies and gives sense to a whole paradigm of values.

As suggested above, the metaphorical process is partial and biased in nature. By activating one among the (or a group of) ready-made patterns (frames, metaphors, narratives, image schemas, prototypes, metonymies) reasoning is unconsciously led to follow *that* scheme, highlighting some aspects and hiding those which do not fit with the path in use without questioning.

It takes a long time for such complex networks to be built up, and as a consequence they cannot be modified overnight. It is a given that we cannot avoid using those paths but this does not suggest there are no possibilities for change. What we can do is become aware of their functioning in order not to be passively influenced by them. Further, since those structures are construed through language, it is also possible to try to change them (or at least to trigger the process of change) starting from language.

Language is a source of evidence for people's conceptual systems. In order to trace the text back to the ideologies which inform it, we will follow the linguistic hints on the surface of discourse: as we have been arguing, linguistic expressions are a "gateway to the mind".

1.3 Yunus's speech: "poverty is a threat to peace".

Muhammad Yunus is a Bangladeshi professor of economics who developed the concepts of microcredit and microfinance: small loans are given to poor people who do not have any guarantee to qualify for traditional bank loans. For this purpose, he founded Grameen Bank, and his efforts have had a relevant impact upon economic and social development. On December 10, 2006, in Oslo, Muhammad Yunus delivered his acceptance speech in behalf of himself and Grameen Bank for the award of the Nobel Peace Prize. His thirty-five-minute Nobel lecture was watched by millions of people from all over the world. After a few words in Bengali, Yunus starts by thanking the Academy for the prestigious prize, thus following the traditional acceptance speech pattern which consists of:

- Initial greetings, acknowledgments and thanks.
- Present situation outline and his/her own activity account.
- Glance at the future, further development and work to do.

Nevertheless, embedded in the "greetings and thanks" *topos* the main conceptual metaphors and moral schemes on the basis of which his entire discourse will be constructed are already introduced. First of all, let us consider some expressions:

remote Bangladeshi villages;

all the way to Oslo.

The distance between Bangladesh and Oslo is clearly emphasized in the contrastive pair here/there, and is also stated in the juxtaposition between all the people who are watching the ceremony on television in Bangladesh and the nine women who are attending the event. What is conveyed here in metaphorical terms is that the gap between poor and rich is a physical one, and the conceptual metaphor underlying it is ECONOMIC DISCREPANCY IS A DISTANCE. The honour of receiving the prize means being recognised, and it is associated with the chance to take part in the event.

By giving their institution the most prestigious prize in the world, you give them unparalleled honour. *Thanks to* your prize, nine proud women from the villages of Bangladesh are at the ceremony today as Nobel laureates, giving an altogether new meaning to the Nobel Peace Prize.

Expressions like "by giving" (which is anaphorically repeated further on) along with "thanks to" stress that *by means* of the Nobel prize the distance has been *shortened*. The physical distance metaphor refers not only to the cultural gap between rich and poor countries, but also to the difficulty for other cultures to "see" what really happens "over there", in Bangladesh. By indirect strategy, Yunus fills up the "greetings and thanks" traditional frame with presuppositional constructions and implicatures which outline the present situation and suggest a different world view. Here presupposition constructions mostly concern existential presupposition:

Nine elected representatives of the 7 million borrowers-cum-owners of Grameen Bank have accompanied me.

(*There are* 7 million people involved with Grameen bank and borrowers *are also* owners)

Nine proud women from the villages of Bangladesh are at the ceremony today.

(Bangladeshi women *are* proud)

This year's prize gives highest honour and dignity to the hundreds of millions of women all around the world who struggle every day to make a living and bring hope for a better life for their children.

(*It is women* who struggle against poverty for themselves and their family and it is so *all around the world*)

Implicatures are more indirect, because they are about what is meant rather than what is said. Let us consider the following passage:

All borrowers of Grameen Bank are celebrating this day as the greatest day of their lives. They are gathering around the nearest television set in their villages all over Bangladesh, along with other villagers, to watch the proceedings of this ceremony.

Yunus is openly flouting the maxims of relevance and quantity (Grice 1975). Actually, the image suggested here is perfectly suited to the subject matter, and serves to introduce his and Grameen bank's world view, a view that is very far from the dominant one in western culture. Since this message is addressed to wealthy societies in which there are three television sets per family on average, it is clearly intended to be striking. At a deeper level, this passage hints at a model of society which will be described in detail later on. In this kind of society social ties must be maintained and attended to, as helping each other is a priority moral duty, according to the "Nurturant family" metaphor which entails that morality is above all social empathy and social nurturance. (Lakoff 1995). Like in the Nurturant Family, in this society women are held in high esteem and play the most important roles. Significantly, the "nine elected representatives" are introduced without specifying their gender, which is revealed only later. By overturning the traditional man-centred "strict father model", which relegates women to subordinate positions, those elected representatives are all women and stand for the hundreds of millions of women responsible for the daily survival of their families.

The second point of the traditional speech pattern concerns the picture of the present worldwide situation. Here the economic outline is said to be strictly linked and in correlation with global peace. "Poverty is a threat to peace". In order to explain this unusual association between poverty and war, Yunus cites figures regarding world income distribution.

Ninety four percent of the world income goes to 40 percent of the population while sixty percent of people live on only 6 per cent of world income.

The use of chiasm forces us to view the same reality from two different points of view, and also underlines the great economic injustice. It is said to be a "telling story". Indeed, there is really a story underlying the next paragraph, a "Rescue Narrative" in which world leaders-heroes decide to join forces and rescue the population-victim from the poverty-villain. "But then came September 11 and the Iraq war" and our heroes are diverted from their mission. According to the conceptual metaphor WAR IS A JOURNEY, the most important *goal* to reduce poverty is *derailed* from the *pursuit* of its aim *shifting* from the war on poverty to the war on terrorism. That is to say, among the difficulties experienced by the hero, there is a "masked" enemy pretending to be the villain and working as a diversion. Our heroes fail to avoid the blunder and waste their efforts in fighting against this enemy.

Till now over $ 530 billion has been spent on the war in Iraq by the USA alone.

This statement implies that an even greater amount of economic effort has been made, but also conveys a slight criticism for the economic paradox, which is, however, forgivable if considered as a result of unwilling and temporary mistaken priorities. This kind of interpretation of events is highly diplomatic, and comes under a strategy of indirectness. It avoids overt criticism and does not reject war as a source domain. Yunus rather suggests a *narrative* in which governments and institutions hold dear poverty issues, but in spite of themselves they have been derailed from the right path.

I believe that putting resources into improving the lives of the poor people is a better strategy than spending it on guns.

The moral accounting scheme Yunus takes position against is Revenge and, as an alternative, he suggests Restitution: the strongest way to fight terrorism is giving poor people their human rights back rather than *buying guns* (which is a metonymy and also a circumlocution for *making war*).

Since morality is universally understood in terms of financial transaction, we can regard peace as a result of the correct bookkeeping of morality and different strategies to achieve peace point to different underlying hierarchies of values. Let us consider some metaphors embedded in the following utterances:

I became involved because poverty was all around me, and I could not turn away from it. (Morality is empathy)

The excitement that was created among the people by this small action got me further involved in it. If I could make so many people so happy with such a tiny amount of money, why not do more of it? (Morality is happiness)

Ninety four percent of the world income goes to 40 percent of the population while sixty percent of people live on only 6 per cent of world income. Half of the world population lives on two dollars a day. Over one billion people live on less than a dollar a day. This is no formula for peace.

Yunus's set of moral priorities is a far cry from that of capitalism and ultimately broader. As Yunus remarks, capitalism claims that "the individual search for personal gains brings collective optimal result". According to Yunus, this is a "one-dimensional" view of human beings, because it only concerns morality as *self*-nurturance, and nurturance is strictly meant as self-*profit*. A few sentences later this economic system is stated to be nonperforming:

Many of the world's problems exist because of this restriction on the players of free-market. The world has not resolved the problem of crushing poverty that half of its population suffers.

Capitalism fails to provide the collective optimal result it had promised because the concept of freedom has been narrowed to individual gain. Again, by means of a diplomatic and indirect strategy, Yunus employs the same schemes used by the "adverse party" without calling into question the validity of the free market system. Yet he works on what we *mean* by freedom:

This interpretation of capitalism insulates the entrepreneurs from all political, emotional, social, spiritual, environmental dimensions of their lives. This was done perhaps as a reasonable simplification, but it stripped away the very essentials of human life.

Peace should be understood in a human way – in a broad social, political and economic way. Peace is threatened by unjust economic, social and political order, absence of democracy, environmental degradation and absence of human rights. Poverty is the absence of all human rights.

Logical steps that lead to the *poverty is a threat to peace* equation are explained here but the last passage is omitted: peace is threatened by the absence of human rights; poverty is the absence of all human rights; *therefore* poverty is a threat to peace. Of course the gap can be easily filled, and the conclusion inferred, but suggesting rather than overtly stating is a more effective strategy for delivering the message. In this passage, everything connected to the lack of nurturance (key words are "unjust", "absence", "degradation") in the fields of the environment, feminism, regulation and multiculturalism is said to be a menace to people. Exactly like a nurturant parent, institutions must protect their children and promote the development of their potential. Since existing institutions do not fulfil this goal, a new type of business is needed. It is called *social business* and Grameen Bank represents an example of this.

Yunus does not dismiss the language and concepts of capitalism, but he rather tries to modify the hearer's structures involved in their understanding. Similar words and phrases here come to be reinterpreted within a different ideological framework. Talking about his new type of business Yunus's strategy consists in employing a modifier – the adjective "social" – which alone totally subverts the traditional profit-maximizing concept associated with business. According to capitalist accounting, the expression "social business" is an oxymoron: there cannot be *non-loss* and *non-dividend* companies in a profit-oriented economy. Hence the prefix *non* does not imply merely the negation of known concepts (i.e. what in rhetoric is called *litotes*), but refers to a new meaning bestowed on the nature and aim of social business. Since it is cost-effective, self-reliant and efficient, social business needs no charitable contribution. Its aim is not making profit but providing "healthcare for the poor, financial services for the poor, information technology for the poor, education and training for the poor, marketing for the poor, renewable energy". As remarked by repetition, it is a poor-oriented business.

It is not charity, because money alone is useless. Trying to solve the problem of poverty is not only a matter of money, it is a matter of *credit*. Poor people are said to be not *creditworthy* by traditional banks («The bank said that the poor were not *creditworthy*»). The latter is a very telling word. Not to be 'worthy of credit' means not to be reliable or trusted. Who *deserves* credit? According to the "Strict father model", poverty is a consequence of laziness and self-indulgence, so since the poor lack discipline, they are immoral and deserve no *credit* (Lakoff 1995). Here Yunus opposes the credit-worthiness language by means of a compound: he states that «Grameen Bank gives *collateral-free* income generating, housing, student and micro-enterprise loans to the poor families». The word *collateral-free* implies the idea that guarantees are a sort of burden or hindrance to the generation of social facilities and thus Grameen Bank stars here as a liberator which thwarts the affliction-cause in a sort of "Rescue-from-affliction" narrative:

I wanted to do something immediate to help people around me [...]. That brought me face to face with poor people's struggle to find the tiniest amounts of money to support their efforts to eke out a living. I was shocked to discover a woman in the village, borrowing less than a dollar from the money-lender, on the *condition* that he would have the *exclusive right* to buy all she produces at the price *he decides*. This, to me, was a way of recruiting *slave labour*. I decided to make a list of the *victims* of *this* money-lending "business" in the village next door to our campus. When my list was done, it had the names of 42 *victims* who borrowed a total amount of US $27. I offered US $27 from my own pocket to get these *victims* out of the *clutches* of *those* money-lenders.

As we can gather from the linguistic expressions in italics, one of the conceptual metaphors underlying Yunus's discourse is MONEY IS POWER (money-lenders establish *conditions*, have *exclusive rights* and make borrowers *slaves*). Combining the MORALITY IS FAIRNESS conceptual metaphor discussed above with MONEY IS POWER we come to another metaphor: MONEY IS FREEDOM. Micro-lending represents a solution to the problem since money (a small amount) allows poor people to break loose from social, economic and political constraints. In other words, poverty is unequal distribution of power, and collateral-free lending represents an opportunity for poor people to gain equal rights. A set of equations are at work here: if *morality* = *wealth* and *morality* = *fairness*, then *social well-being* = *fair distribution of wealth*. Moreover, since people who possess money hold the power, *equal opportunities for everyone* = *economic freedom*. The compound *slave labour* is a common metonymy in economic language. The modifier (slave) is attributed to the action (labour) instead of denoting the agent (worker), and it literally means that the poor are exploited and made slaves *by* unjust labour conditions. Labour here refers to workers, to their work and to its economic value at the same time, as if men and women were *one-dimensional* human beings only dedicated to work in their lives. That is another way to say that capitalism sets limits to human potential. The following simile is consistent with this ideological frame:

To me poor people are like bonsai trees. When you plant the best seed of the tallest tree in a flower-pot, you get a replica of the tallest tree, only inches tall. There is nothing wrong with the seed you planted, only the soil-base that is too inadequate. Poor people are bonsai people. There is nothing wrong in their seeds. Simply, society never gave them the base to grow on.

Poverty is described as a physical constraint imposed by capitalism:

Many of the world's problems exist because of this *restriction* on the players of free-market. The world has not resolved the problem of *crushing* poverty that half of its population *suffers*.

Poor people today are confined to *tiny* rooms which seem to be *far* from the world's riches (cf. the ECONOMIC DISCREPANCY IS A DISTANCE conceptual metaphor discussed above) . Those who have been *reached* with microcredit have *crossed* the poverty *line*. In this sense Information and

Communication Technology is seen as a means of shortening the distance:

Information and communication technology (ICT) is quickly changing the world, creating *distanceless, borderless* world of instantaneous communications. Increasingly, it is becoming less and less costly. I saw an opportunity for the poor people to change their lives if this technology could be *brought* to them to *meet* their needs.

Yunus's discourse largely revolves around the narrow/broad contrastive pair, in which *narrow* represents the negative pole (everything constraining, oppressing, reducing) while *broad* stands for positive values such as growth, social relationships and free expression. Nevertheless, the absolute economic freedom of globalization without regulation is likely to prove to be unequal for its participants:

I support globalization and believe it can bring more benefits to the poor than its alternative. But it must be the right kind of globalization. To me, globalization is like a hundred-lane highway criss-crossing the world. If it is a free-for-all highway, its lanes will be taken over by the giant trucks from powerful economies. Bangladeshi rickshaw will be *thrown off* the highway. In order to have a *win-win* globalization we must have traffic rules, traffic police, and traffic authority for this global highway. Rule of "strongest takes it all" must be replaced by rules that ensure that the poorest have a place and piece of the action, without being *elbowed out* by the strong. Globalization must not become financial imperialism.

Economy is here described in terms of *race*: someone elbows, others are thrown off the road and there are winners and losers. *Win-win* is a business language expression that describes a negotiation outcome in which both parties benefit. Experience shows that win-win solution needs some planning prior to the negotiation: on a worldwide scale regulation is essential in order to avoid uneven competition. The concept of equality is assigned a further meaning here: differentiated conditions must be set in order to meet different needs and to give equal opportunities. Through the highway simile Yunus connects two domains: the free market and the circulation of traffic. Since rules and supervising authorities are undisputed and perfectly consistent with the latter domain, by means of association it sounds reasonable and *natural* to provide these controlling institutions also for free market.

Yunus's last considerations regard proposals, plans, purposes and dreams, so that verb tenses accordingly shift from present/past to the future simple tense. At the same time, the pronoun "we" is subject to a denotational shift: earlier referred to Yunus and Grameen Bank, "we" now addresses all the people of the world including companies, new generations and ordinary people. Flexibility of deixis is taken advantage of in order to broaden and to foreground collective responsibility for still existent poverty.

We get *what we want*, or what we don't refuse. [...] If we firmly believe that poverty is unacceptable to us, and that it should not belong to a civilized society, we would have built appropriate institutions and policies to create a poverty-free world. *We wanted* to go to the moon, so we went there. We achieve *what we want* to achieve. If we are not achieving something, it is because we have not put our *minds* to it. We create *what we want*. *What we want* and how we get to it depends on our *mindsets*. It is extremely difficult to change *mindsets* once they are formed. We create the world in accordance with our *mindset*. We need to invent ways to change our perspective continually and *reconfigure* our *mindset* quickly as new knowledge emerges. We can *reconfigure* our world if we can *reconfigure* our *mindset*.

Yunus demonstrates that new mental schemes are formed (and old ones are modified) chiefly through language. In this passage key words are repeated many times (*mindset, reconfigure, want*). This is a kind of *metatextual* procedure in which Yunus explains the importance of changing our mindset *by means of* the most powerful strategy for reconfiguring these mental patterns: repetition.

1.4 Jobs's speech: about connecting the dots.

On June 12, 2005, Steve Jobs, at that time the CEO of Apple and Pixar animation, delivered his commencement speech at Stanford University. It was very hot and the students were fanning themselves, while a plane flew over the ceremony with a banner reading: "Steve, don't be a mini-player—recycle all e-waste".

Just one sentence is allotted by Jobs to initial greetings, acknowledgments and thanks, and what follows is delivered in informal and conversational style through the use of paratactic structures, phrasal verbs, short sentences, repetition, and so on, in order to increase the newly graduated young students' receptiveness to his message.

I am honored to be with you today at your commencement from one of the finest universities in the world. Truth be told, I never graduated from college. This is the closest I've ever gotten to a college graduation. Today I want to tell you three stories from my life. That's it. No big deal. Just three stories.

By saying "truth be told" Jobs introduces his intention to "get naked". On the stage there is himself and his personal life. He shows humility and he plays the role of a father: he wants to provide his children with *telling* life stories which, like *exempla,* will teach them the essential things about life. As a statement of style, what follows is said not to be a "big deal", but *just* three stories. Simplicity, clarity and systematic insight are the stylistic and conceptual features Jobs wants to foreground.

According to these features, the entire speech pivots on "the rule of three". This rule informs both the text structure as a whole and its parts, as well as its themes. Following tradition, three are the sequences the speech pattern consists of (cf. above). The central part of the speech is also structured into three, the same number as the stories which are told: the first is about connecting the dots, the second is about love and loss, and the last is about death. Moreover, the rule of three, often combined with anaphora, is applied to many sentences and phrases throughout the speech:

- "**Every** poster, **every** label on **every** drawer was beautifully hand calligraphed."
- "I learned [1] **about** serif and san serif typefaces, [2] **about** varying the amount of space between different letter combinations, [3] **about** what makes great typography great."
- "It was [1] beautiful, [2] historical, [3] artistically subtle."
- "[1] started a company named NeXT, [2] another company named Pixar, [3] and fell in love."
- "[1] **all** external expectations, [2] **all** pride, [3] **all** fear."
- "[1] **It means to** try to tell your kids everything you thought you'd have the next ten years to tell them in just a few months. [2] **It means to** make sure everything is buttoned up so that it will be as easy as possible for your family. [3] **It means to** say your goodbyes."
- [1] **don't** waste it living someone else's life. [2] **Don't** be trapped by dogma […] [3] **Don't** let the noise of others' opinions drown out your own inner voice."

Finally, three are also the stages of human existence the speech refers to: life, death and re-birth. Here are some examples of the metaphorical reference to the "circle of life" concept:

- In Jobs's college career, *dropping in* is followed by *dropping out* and by *dropping in* again. The "death" of his formal academic career makes way for the "birth" of his informal learning process.

- Jobs *gives birth* to Apple which *grows*. Later, when Apple buys NeXT, Apple experiences a *"renaissance"* that implies its previous death.

- The «Whole Earth Catalog» *is brought to life* by Stewart Brand, then it *runs its course* and it gets to its *final issue*, but it *revives* again in Jobs's quote.

Things that come in threes are inherently and commonly perceived as more satisfying, more effective and more easily memorable. But besides rhetorical implications, their use here is more significantly linked to the underlying ideology of the speech. The three-structure traditionally conveys the idea of completeness and perfection and it suggests that there might not be anything else besides what is outlined in the threes, so that things and happenings are seen as already settled. In fact, at whatever level it is applied, the "rule of three" in Jobs's speech is strictly connected to the teleological conception of life, namely the belief that events have an ultimate end, a predetermined purpose or design, whoever may be the Designer, and they are not casual. As he says at the end of the first story, understanding the design is a matter of *trust* in the connection of the dots:

Of course it was impossible to connect the dots looking forward when I was in college. But it was very, very clear looking backwards ten years later.

Again, you can't connect the dots looking forward; you can only connect them looking backwards. So you have to trust that the dots will somehow connect in your future. You have to trust in something — your gut, destiny, life, karma, whatever.

The way things will connect is unfathomable at the present time because the complex design can be understood only in retrospect. Jobs's account is told from the perspective of an omniscient narrator, i.e. from the privileged position of who has finally connected the dots. Besides the rule of threes, teleological conception is conveyed by a few narrative strategies regarding the plot arrangement, syntactic structures and *narratives*. Let us examine them in detail.

Jobs often plays with the plot by bringing the outcome of events forward and filling the gap in the intermediate events with a flashback. Here are two examples. In the first story, Jobs accounts for having dropped out of college and a rhetorical question is followed by a flashback:

I dropped out of Reed College after the first 6 months, but then stayed around as a drop-in for another 18 months or so before I really quit. So why did I drop out? It started before I was born. [...]

In the second story, Jobs accounts for his layoff at the peak of his career. Again, through a flashback:

We had just released our finest creation — the Macintosh — a year earlier, and I had just turned 30. And then I got fired. How can you get fired from a company you started? Well, as Apple grew we hired someone [...]

In the third story there is an implicit flash forward since it is clear that the doctors were wrong with their death sentence: Jobs was still alive.

All these manipulations of chronological structure foreground Jobs's end-oriented view of life which informs the speech: what happened later explains and justifies *how* he got there. Accordingly, the third-conditional syntactic structures emphasize the unavoidability of destiny:

If I had never dropped in on that single course in college, the Mac would have never had multiple typefaces or proportionally spaced fonts. And since Windows just copied the Mac, it's likely that no personal computer would have them. If I had never dropped out, I would have never dropped in on this calligraphy class, and personal computers might not have the wonderful typography that they do.

What is implied here is that only *that* course of events could have led to the present situation. In a certain sense, everything was already written in a constellation of dots.

Finally, predetermination of events is also suggested by and embedded into the *narratives* on which the three stories are shaped. Jobs was born as an unexpected and unwanted baby and he was adopted by working-class parents who could barely afford his tuition. He goes through many ups and downs and hit-and-miss experiences. Thanks to his hard work and wit, he eventually succeeds in becoming a billionaire. The pattern of Jobs's story follows each and every point the Rags-to-Riches – or Pull-Yourself-up-by-your-Bootstraps – narrative which "itself is an American icon, defining a version of the American dream, what every American who starts out poor should – and could – be doing." (Lakoff 2008: 29). Reinvention-of-the-Self narrative is also activated here: after getting fired with dishonour, Jobs decides to *start over* and create a new company (significantly) called NeXT. Being based on ready-made mental patterns, it is as if Jobs's life story was virtually already written. By following narrative patterns, no other outcome but the expected one is possible.

Teleological conception traditionally entails performing actions which must be oriented towards *good*, regardless of their consequences. The conception of good is by definition the source of moral value. But what is the ultimate end that events are aimed at in Jobs's discourse? The answer might be found in Jobs's conclusions. In fact each story is followed by a moral lesson that bestows universal validity on the personal experience recounted. These lessons are conveyed through positive and negative imperatives as well as obligations (have to/must), as follows:

So *you have to trust* that the dots will somehow connect in your future. [...] Because believe in the dots connect *down the road* will give you the confidence to follow your *heart* even when it leads you off the *well-worn* path and that would make all the *difference*.

Don't lose faith. [...] *You've got to find what you love.* [...] Your work is going to fill a large part of your life, and the only way to be truly satisfied is to do what you believe is great work. And the only way to do great work is to *love* what you do. If you haven't found it yet, keep looking. *Don't settle.* [...] So keep looking until you find it. *Don't settle.*

Your time is limited, so *don't waste it* living *someone else's life. Don't be trapped* by dogma — which is living with the results of *other people's* thinking. *Don't let the noise of others' opinions drown out your own inner voice.* And most important, have the courage to follow your *heart* and intuition. […] Everything else is secondary.

Some observations can be made. First, these *rules* for success state that succeeding in life is an *individual* matter. The rules are also given moral value in that their aim consists in achieving personal well-being: being successful is a necessary condition for being happy. Consistent with this, the first person pronoun dominates the entire text and the subjective account easily shifts from individual experience to universal values: what proved true for him is posited as a set of *rules* for success and happiness. Moreover, identity is determined *by the difference* between the self and other people.

Secondly, freedom is achieved through individual economic initiative and community (other people) is seen as an obstacle (a *noise*, a *trap*) which must be overcome or avoided. Moreover, as the TIME IS MONEY metaphor is at work here, *spending* time with other people's ideas is equivalent to *wasting* time.

Finally, starting from the second story (about love and loss) the business domain is associated to love relationships. And since business is meant as individual initiative, thus love seems to be interpreted as love for the self. Let us see in detail how love is conceptually expanded throughout the speech. Below are all the linguistic expressions referring to heart and love in the BUSINESS IS A PARTNER conceptual metaphor.

Heart:

The technology we developed at NeXT is at the *heart* of Apple's current renaissance.

As with all matters of the *heart*, you'll know when you find it.

There is no reason not to follow your *heart*.

And most important, have the courage to follow your *heart* and intuition.

Love:

I found what I *loved* to do early in life.

I still *loved* what I did.

I had been rejected, but I was still in *love*.

I'm convinced that the only thing that kept me going was that I *loved* what I did. You've got to find what you *love*. And that is as true for your work as it is for your *lovers*.

And the only way to do great work is to *love* what you do.

According to this, love means devoting oneself to work, which in turn is aimed at maximizing profit. But capitalizing is more than an object of desire. It is felt as an inherited moral duty:

So at 30 I was out. And very publicly out. What had been the focus of my entire adult life was gone, and it was devastating. I really didn't know what to do for a few months. I felt that I had let the previous generation of entrepreneurs down - that I had dropped the baton as it was being passed to me.

Furthermore, if we consider that succeeding in "what you love to do" is here evaluated in terms of money and number of employees («We worked hard, and in 10 years Apple had grown from just the two of us in a garage into a $2 billion company with over 4000 employees») and since «like any great relationship, it just gets better and better as the years roll on», then the increase in profit is seen as to be unbounded.

Everything else is secondary.

Success at work seems to be a necessary condition for being successful in other fields.

During the next five years, I started a company named NeXT, another company named Pixar, *and* fell in love with an amazing woman who would become my wife. Pixar went on to create the worlds first computer animated feature film, Toy Story, and is now the most successful animation studio in the world. In a remarkable turn of events, Apple bought NeXT, I returned to Apple, and the technology we developed at NeXT is at the heart of Apple's current renaissance. *And* Laurene and I have a wonderful family together.

The conjunction *and* first connects the start of NeXt with Jobs's engagement and then the fortunate turn of events with the start of Jobs's family. In the two pairs of events utterances order and & conjunction suggest there is likely to be an implicit *as a result*, i.e. a causal connection between the two events (cf. Bach 2006: 479-480). What is suggested here is that Jobs's successful marriage is entailed by, or comes as an implicature from (cf. Horn 2006: 18), the successful outcome of his business.

According to tradition, in the conclusion Jobs glances at the future and gives some advice which sums up the ideology interwoven in his three stories. For this purpose, he tells another story. This time it is about Stewart Brand and his publication *"The Whole Earth Catalog*, which was one of the bibles of [Job's] generation". Jobs quotes the farewell message written in the final issue and addresses it to Stanford students: stay hungry, stay foolish. There is a cluster of rhetorical figures in this simple sentence: anaphora, parallelism, metaphor and antithesis. The verb "stay" presupposes that the audience is *already* hungry and foolish, as if this was an inherent human attitude, at least inherent to youth. In fact the verb "stay" entails that, if not cultivated, hunger and foolishness tend to fade. The adjective "hungry" refers to a craving, a strong desire which reminds us of the strong love feeling described in the second story. Thus Jobs's advice – stay hungry - comes under the wider BUSINESS IS A PARTNER conceptual metaphor and is another way to say "don't settle", either in love affairs or in business, because just as great relationships get "better and better as the years roll on" so economic initiative must be aimed at maximizing profit.

On the other hand, the adjective foolish refers to the naive and inquiring attitude typical of the new and untried generation who often acts instinctively without taking into account the advice of older and more experienced people.

The adjective "foolish" seems to be the antithesis of "hungry", in that are reminiscent of the contrastive pair lightness/heaviness which is posited in the second story: "the lightness of being a beginner" versus "the heaviness of being successful". Moreover, being foolish stands for daring to make unconventional decisions which lead off the "*well-worn* path and that would make all the *difference*". In fact according to this account, as discussed above, individual concern is put into the foreground since the secret of success lies in not following well-worn patterns, which means standing out from the crowd.

Not surprisingly, in 1997 Apple Inc. chose an advertising slogan which was heavily publicized through TV promos and print advertisements and that sums up Jobs's philosophy: *think different.*

Chapter 3:
WE ARE AT WAR: ADDRESSING THE NATION,
King George VI's and Roosevelt's Speeches

2.1   Theoretical background, tools of analysis and aims.

This paper will explore a particular sub-genre of political discourse – the declaration of war – focusing on two addresses to their nation by western leaders – King George VI and US President Franklin D. Roosevelt – through which citizens are informed about the new conflict. These speeches belong to two historic moments – the entrance into World War II of the United Kingdom and the United States (1939 and 1941) – in which western identity was felt to be at risk. Unlike (and far more interesting than) the formal written or spoken declarations of war which usually precede them, addresses to the nation are in-group oriented and their aim comprises a wide range of illocutionary speech acts: not only declarations, but also representatives, expressives, commissives, rogatives and directives (Searle 1975). In other words, by announcing the future war to the nation, the political leader at the same time reassures, issues orders, expresses empathy, informs about the state of affairs, makes promises, and so on.

Declaring war is always a critical political action to be taken by political leadership. What is primarily under attack is the nation's cohesion itself. War is in fact probably the most undesirable and destabilizing event in the life of a nation: it brings violence, death, social disruption, and economic recession. No citizens would want to face such consequences and going from a time of peace to a time of war can be a very difficult thing to persuade the public to support. Pro-war addresses have one key characteristic in common: propaganda. This concept, which has progressively gained a negative connotation, can be defined as the deliberate attempt by an individual or a group of people «to influence the opinions, attitudes and behaviour of a person, a group of persons, or the masses […] predominantly by means of directive persuasive techniques» with the intention to reach a certain ends (De Wet 2010). Therefore in these speeches, whether it is true or not that the nation is undergoing attacks from outside enemies and whatever its true aim is, war is *presented* as a necessary response to whoever or whatever threatens the political system, its values and institutions. In other words, in these addresses the underlying strategy of political leadership consists in strengthening consensus by appealing to those principles, values and duties which together define the interests of the group and which are shared by all the members of the nation. It means enhancing and orienting *political cognition*, i.e. «shared knowledge and political attitudes» otherwise defined as «public opinion», through political discourse (Van Dijk 1997: 18).

Following Van Dijk's account on political-critical discourse analysis (1995, 1997), the following analyses aim at highlighting the structures and strategies of the speeches which involve topics, textual schemata, local semantics, lexicon, syntax, and rhetoric. Finally I will examine expression structures, speech acts and interaction in order to show how these speeches are defined by and contribute to reinforcing the "ideological square", i.e. «the basic belief systems that underlie and organize the shared social representations of groups and their members». Finally, Lakoff's insight into cognitive metaphors and moral accounting schemes will be taken into consideration as regards the justification of war and its moral implications (1995).

To some extent these speeches might be considered as a "manifesto" of western identity which echoes and accounts for shared western values such as democracy, freedom, independence, rights, loyalty, security and justice. I will attempt to show that, since the nation's identity is in danger, the polarization between ingroups and outgroups (i.e. the contraposition between US and THEM which defines and organizes the ideology) is dramatically emphasized and foregrounded, while on the other hand, all the *internal* boundaries among social and political subgroups are cut across in the name of a higher membership: that of the nation.

2.2   King George VI's speech: the right thing.

On September 3, 1939 King George VI broadcast a six-minute speech to his people in Britain and throughout the Empire, immediately after Britain's Declaration of War against Germany.

The main topic is obviously the recent political events and action (the war), but far more interesting is how in King George's speech this topic is modalized (presented as regretted but necessary) and evaluated (by the polarization between WE and THEY) by the speaker. Let us start from the opening sentence.

In this grave hour, perhaps the most fateful in our history, I send to every household of my peoples, both at home and overseas, this message, spoken with the same depth of feeling for each one of you as if I were able to cross your threshold and speak to you myself.

According to Jacobson's categorization of language functions (Jacobson 1960), we might say that the first sentence combines *phatic* and *conative* functions since the message refers to all the listeners the speech addresses, both near and far, and at the same time is intended to "cross their threshold" as if the communication channel was being checked.

However, the *referential* (contextual information) and *emotive* (self-expression) functions also play an important role here. In fact the context of the overall utterance is described through a prepositional phrase («in this grave hour») which is followed by a parenthetical modification («perhaps the most fateful in our history»). The present time is depicted as the most difficult and challenging ever: the hour is said to be *grave* and *fateful*, and both adjectives activate the semantic field of death, implying also a crucial and uncertain outcome of the future events. As regards the emotive function, in this second part of the sentence information is added about the *way* the message is uttered rather than explicating what the message is about, that is to say the focus is on the speaker's attitude towards the message itself. The direct object «this message» is followed by a participle clause («spoken with..») which in turn introduces an adverb clause («as if I were..»). The addresser wants to express his great empathy and emotional nearness to his peoples, and hypotactic structure conveys the speaker's (actual or pretended) difficulty in articulating his message due to the seriousness of the situation. The effects of this linguistic strategy provide an appearance of direct concern and contact with each member of English people, and matches what Norman Fairclough, in *Language and Power* (1989), defines as "synthetic personalization", i.e. «a compensatory tendency to give the impression of treating each of the people 'handled' *en masse* as an individual» (Fairclough 1989: 62). Moreover, by expressing his nearness to «each one of you», King George lays the ground for the directives he will give at the end of the speech and which will appeal to individual responsibility.

The second sentence conveys the main topic of the overall message: "we are at war". Primacy is given to the acknowledgment of the fact that it is the *second* war, at a short distance from the first, and in so doing George VI shows empathy with British people for how they must have felt. Since a direct connection between "I" and "my peoples" has been established, the subject now shifts from I to an inclusive WE which consequently refers to the King, the Government and everybody in the Commonwealth. But immediately after, while summarizing the futile attempts of peace negotiation, the pronoun WE shifts again to a restrictive use.

Over and over again we have tried to find a peaceful way out of the differences between ourselves and those who are now our enemies. But it has been in vain. We have been forced into a conflict.

That is to say, war has been declared and managed by the government, but it will affect and involve all the subjects. Nevertheless, the differences between the group actors (the government, the King and the subjects) are blurred, and the deictic WE easily shifts from referring to the political leadership to indicating the nation as a whole. This can be regarded as a linguistic strategy which aims at enhancing and improving ingroup cohesion.

By following the same strategy, the polarization between WE and THEY is strengthened: as regards the responsibilities and the motivations which led to the conflict, a positive self-presentation and a negative other-presentation is given. Great Britain and its allies (WE) are depicted as peace makers since they have done their utmost to avoid war. The expression «those who are now our enemies» entails that THEY have not collaborated in peace negotiation. As a consequence, it is said that «we have been forced into a conflict» and «we are called [...] to meet the challenge». These passive constructions, along with the lexical choice of the verb "to force", the responsibility of the others for war versus "our" role as victims.

Significantly, Germany and its allies are not explicitly mentioned, but loosely described as "those", "our enemies", and are identified with that evil principle which menaces the freedom and values of the Commonwealth of Nations as well as western identity itself.

For we are called, with our allies, to meet the challenge of a principle which, if it were to prevail, would be fatal to any civilised order in the world.

The conditional clause «if it were to prevail» is put into parenthetical position as if the possibility of being defeated should be dreaded but not taken seriously into consideration. Moreover, in this statement Great Britain's defeat would imply the end of any form of civilization virtually all around the world: it entails not only that the enemies are *not* civilised, but also that Great Britain will play a central role in saving the world (the allies are only mentioned parenthetically).

Enemies and their evil actions are described through the principle they conform to:

It is the principle which permits a state, in the selfish pursuit of power, to disregard its treaties and its solemn pledges; which sanctions the use of force, or threat of force, against the sovereignty and independence of other states. Such a principle, stripped of all disguise, is surely the mere primitive doctrine that might is right; and if this principle were established throughout the world, the freedom of our own country and of the whole British Commonwealth of Nations would be in danger. But far more than this - the peoples of the world would be kept in the bondage of fear, and all hopes of settled peace and of the security of justice and liberty among nations would be ended.

The strategy at work here is referred to as "functional relation of Generalization" (Van Dijk 1997: 32), and consists in presenting the bad actions of opponents as typical of the Others and in blurring the boundaries between the individual identities of outgroup members. THEY are seen en bloc (rather than as individuals), and (by means of further generalization) THEY ultimately coincide with the principle that their political leadership complies with. That principle is obviously said to be an evil one, so that if THEY were to prevail, the scenario which would ensue from the defeat is depicted as an apocalyptic one: people kept in the bondage of fear, no hope and the end of any form of civilization.

In a certain sense, arguing about the "principle" in place of people is also a *disclaimer*, «which is a semantic move that aims at avoiding a bad impression when saying negative things about Others» (Van Dijk 1997: 32). Rather than directly asserting that THEY are selfish, overbearing, only concerned with power and disrespectful of vows, word of honour and international agreements, while WE are fair, peaceable and loyal, the polarization between WE on one hand and THEY on the other is respectively shifted to that between civilization and savagery, that is between the "high purpose" and the evil "principle". The "high purpose" consists in the defence of the values of western democracies, and these values are referred to through a list of key words, placed in polysyndetic coordination, which encompasses «all that we ourselves hold dear»: freedom, peace, security, justice, liberty, sovereignty and independence. WE fight for those values and ultimately WE *are* those values.

At this point of the speech, a litotes focuses again on the non-feasibility and unavoidability of war, which is euphemistically defined as a challenge:

it is unthinkable that we should refuse to meet the challenge.

This statement mirrors a concept already expressed at the beginning: «we are called [...] to meet the challenge». Nevertheless, it is important to remark that, contrary to what happens in mathematics, in pragmatics a double negative does not have the same effect and implication as the corresponding affirmative sentence. This litotes is a more indirect way to say "we have to make war" and we might argue that the speaker's intent is to convince the listener to support war by negating any alternative. Moreover, the decision is presented here as if it has not already been made, thus pretending to involve actively the listeners in the decision-making process.

In the last part of the speech, the speaker's intentions become more explicit through the use of two performative utterances, i.e. utterances that contain a performative verb and explicitly describe the intended speech act (Austin 1976):

It is to this high purpose that *I now call* my people at home and my peoples across the seas, who will make our cause their own. *I ask* them to stand calm, firm, and united in this time of trial.

Both performatives are directives since they are intended to cause the listener to take a particular action. There is an interesting shift in the use of pronouns here: «my people» is no longer included in the extensive use of the pronoun we, but rather referred to as THEM. We might interpret this as follows: after having established a direct contact with his peoples in the introduction, and having reinforced their consent throughout the argumentation, now George VI restores political roles and orders his subjects (them) to stay calm, firm and united. Through a relative clause, he also presupposes that they «will make our cause their own».

George VI's strategy is also aimed at reassuring British people by showing resoluteness.

we can only do the right as we see the right.

This parallelism and epiphora expresses the King's resolute attitude and conveys the idea of a direct connection between thought and action. Since *do the right* here is synonymous with *to make war*, this clause also presupposes that the country is on the side of right in the conflict.

Victory is presented as subordinated to cohesion around the ideological square as well as to God's help (mentioned in a parenthetical clause) and the war, earlier defined as a *challenge*, a *cause* and *the right*, now is referred to as a *task* and a *time of trial*.

The task will be hard. There may be dark days ahead, and war can no longer be confined to the battlefield. But we can only do the right as we see the right, and reverently commit our cause to God. If one and all we keep resolutely faithful to it, ready for whatever service or sacrifice it may demand, then, with God's help, we shall prevail.

George VI is now outlining the "dark side" of war, but he mitigates the topic by using modal verbs (may, can, will) and litotes («war can no longer be confined to the battlefield»).

In conclusion, the conflict is chiefly presented as an ideological one, since the two opponents, WE and THEY, are related to a "high purpose" and to an evil "principle" respectively, and through a semantic strategy the enemies «get short thrift, remain implicit or referred to only indirectly or vaguely» (Van Dijk 1997: 31). In order to strengthen consent, the King calls on his subjects to gather around the ideological square. Moreover, he presents war as regrettable but unavoidable by modalizing the topic through a cluster of linguistic strategies, such as primacy and recency, presuppositions, indirectness, the use of pronouns, rhetorical figures and so on. In doing so, any opposition to the war cause is made ineffective and "unthinkable".

2.3   Roosevelt's speech: winning the war to win the peace.

On the morning of December 7, 1941, the Japanese navy conducted a surprise military strike on the United States naval base at Pearl Harbour. The following day, US President Franklin Delano Roosevelt delivered a speech before Congress, known as "the infamy speech", and war on Japan was declared.

On the evening of December 9, Roosevelt gave one of his "fireside chats", a series of radio addresses to the nation broadcast between 1933 and 1945 during which the President used to talk to American citizens in a more direct and intimate way than he could do on formal occasions. That evening, of course, the topic was the declaration of war with Japan.

From the first sentence, the enemy is evaluated and recent events are included in a broader framework of time and space:

The sudden criminal attacks perpetrated by the Japanese in the Pacific provide the climax of a decade of international immorality.

The Japanese are indirectly referred to as criminal and immoral, and the attacks they "perpetrated" are said to be the culmination of a decade which will be characterized by increasing («climax») and widespread («international») violence. The same indirect strategy of evaluation is complied with throughout the speech: according to a well-known move which has been already defined as a disclaimer (Van Dijk 1997: 32), vilifying terms such as "criminals", "gangsters", "gangsterism", "aggressors" and "bandits" are usually referred to actions, principles, strategies or phrases like "the enemies" and not directly attributed to Japan or other nations in the same sentence. However, at a short distance (usually in the following sentence) Japan, or Germany, or any of the Axis members are mentioned according to what might be considered a cataphoric pattern, so that the listener inevitably associates the previous negative evaluation with the Axis powers. The following is one example:

Powerful and resourceful gangsters have banded together to make war upon the whole human race. Their challenge has now been flung at the United States of America. The Japanese have treacherously violated the long-standing peace between us.

Throughout the speech, extensive use of anaphora and epiphora is made. Repetition usually affects the salient points of argumentation, thereby lending them emphasis. Their use is obviously aimed at appealing to pathos and also at inspiring motivation by heightening intensity. In the first part of the speech, anaphora and epiphora serve to build and strengthen the polarization between the two opponents, i.e. between WE and THEY.

Many American soldiers and sailors have been killed by enemy action. American ships have been sunk; American airplanes have been destroyed.

In these passive constructions, the object's nationality is highlighted by anaphora. Compared with more neutral ways of referring to casualties and damages, the repetition of "American" is aimed at arousing patriotism and anger among American listeners. Conversely, shared «treacherous» *modus operandi* of the enemies is pointed out through the use of epiphora.

In 1931, ten years ago, Japan invaded Manchukuo—without warning.

In 1935, Italy invaded Ethiopia—without warning.

In 1938, Hitler occupied Austria —without warning.

In 1939, Hitler invaded Czechoslovakia- without warning.

Later in 1939, Hitler invaded Poland- without warning.

In 1940, Hitler invaded Norway, Denmark, the Netherlands, Belgium, and Luxembourg- without warning.

In 1940, Italy attacked France and later Greece—without warning.

And this year, in 1941, the Axis powers attacked Yugoslavia and Greece and they dominated the Balkans—without warning. In 1941, also, Hitler invaded Russia—without warning.

And now Japan has attacked Malaya and Thailand—and the United States— without warning.

In fact, a detailed excursus of THEIR military action is given and each and every one of the ten listed events is followed by the repetition of «without warning». The pattern of both content and syntactic form always remains the same: date, subject (one of the Axis members), verb (invade/occupy/attack/dominate), object and then the expression «without warning». Parallelism conveys the idea that «it is all of one pattern»: namely, not only Japan, but Germany and Italy are enemies in a conflict which is taking place on worldwide scale («the most tremendous undertaking of our American history»).

The magnitude of war is emphasized through enumeratio and polysyndeton which create a sense of being overwhelmed:

The attack at Pearl Harbor can be repeated at any one of many points, points in both oceans and along both our coast lines and against all the rest of the hemisphere.

The production must be not only for our own Army and Navy and Air Forces. It must reinforce the other armies and navies and air forces fighting the Nazis and the war lords of Japan throughout the Americas and throughout the world.

Accordingly, the increase in production by war industry is also described by enumeratio, in order to reassure citizens about US military preparation.

Assembly lines are now in operation. Others are being rushed to completion. A steady stream of tanks and planes, of guns and ships, and shells and equipment [...].

Enemies are said to be «crafty and powerful» and they are almost praised for their ability through an "apparent concession" (Van Dijk 1997: 32):

We may acknowledge that our enemies have performed a brilliant feat of deception, perfectly timed and executed with great skill.

Consequently, it is predicted that the war will be a long and difficult one. All this emphasis on the difficulty of the task to be faced might be considered a preparatory move for the requests that will follow. In fact, since it will be a hard global conflict, «every single man, woman, and child» must play their part. The list of duties and privations that citizens will have to face is introduced by a paralipsis, a device used to introduce a subject by claiming not to do so:

I was about to add that ahead there lies sacrifice for all of us. But it is not correct to use that word.

Then, the main (matrix) clause «it is not a sacrifice» is anaphorically repeated and each time it embeds non-finite clauses which describe all the things American people will have to do or all the things they will have to do without:

It is not a sacrifice for any man, old or young, to be in the Army or the Navy of the United States. Rather is it a privilege. It is not a sacrifice for the industrialist or the wage earner, the farmer or the shopkeeper, the trainman or the doctor, to pay more taxes, to buy more bonds, to forego extra profits, to work longer or harder at the task for which he is best fitted. Rather is it a privilege. It is not a sacrifice to do without many things to which we are accustomed if the national defense calls for doing without.

The indirect illocutionary speech act underlying these statements is an *order*, but the syntactic and rhetorical form lend the locution a much more persuasive and convincing force. It becomes apparent that along with the compliance of citizens, the President also angles for their consent and willingness to accomplish their duties. Therefore, he suggests what they are supposed to do according to the American ideological square through contrastive meanings: sacrifice is opposed to privilege, and while the former is negated and repeated at the beginning of each paragraph, the latter is repeated at the end.

The "embedding strategy" is employed repeatedly throughout the speech. These syntactic structures feature a reversal of the position of topic and comment: first, the topical position is filled by comment, while the topic is backgrounded and sometimes presented as a given. In the following statements, for example, the main (matrix) clause expresses (the subject's) opinion and it embeds a noun clause which conveys the topic of the sentence, i.e. what the opinion is about:

And I am sure that the people in every part of the Nation are prepared in their individual living to win this war. I am sure that they will cheerfully help to pay a large part of its financial cost while it goes on. I am sure they will cheerfully give up those material things that they are asked to give up.

And I am sure that they will retain all those great spiritual things without which we cannot win through.

I do not think any American has any doubt of our ability to administer proper punishment to the perpetrators of these crimes.

In these fragments, the focus is on the subject's degree of certainty rather than on the opinion content, and this partly prevents the addressees from resisting the embedded arguments or at least from verifying their truth value.

Elsewhere it is factive expressions of the main clause (mostly modalized as a necessity or a strong recommendation) which embed dependent clauses. And again, embedded clauses convey the topic:

Your Government knows that for weeks Germany has been telling Japan that if Japan did not attack the United States, Japan would not share in dividing the spoils with Germany when peace came.

American people must realize that it [the Axis powers' strategy] can be matched only with similar grand strategy. We must realize for example that Japanese successes against the United States in the Pacific are helpful to German operations in Libya; that any German success against the Caucasus is inevitably an assistance to Japan in her operations against the Dutch East Indies; that a German attack against Algiers or Morocco opens the way to a German attack against South America, and the Canal.

We must learn also to know that guerrilla warfare against the Germans in, let us say, Serbia or Norway helps us; that a successful Russian offensive against the Germans helps us; and that British successes on land or sea in any part of the world strengthen our hands.

It must be remembered by each and every one of us that our free and rapid communication these days must be greatly restricted in wartime.

We must never forget what we have learned. And what we all have learned is this [...]. We have learned that our ocean-girt hemisphere is not immune from severe attack—that we cannot measure our safety in terms of miles on any map any more.

By topicalizing and fronting the comment, the topic that follows is presupposed rather than discussed. As Van Dijk argues, «presuppositions may have prominent ideological functions in discourse. Precisely because they pertain to knowledge or other beliefs that are not asserted, but simply assumed to be true by the speaker, they are able to 'introduce' ideological propositions whose truth is not uncontroversial at all. As in the case for implications, they allow speakers or writers to make claims without actually asserting them, and, moreover, take specific beliefs for granted although they might not be» (Van Dijk 1995: 273).

Factive verbs such as "realize", "know", "learn", "remember" and "forget" usually require what follows be true. Among others, the following propositions are presupposed in the utterances above:

- aggressive war is the only feasible and rational response to an aggressive attack;
- Germany wants to attack South America;
- Axis's enemies are our allies;
- as a consequence to Japanese attack, American people don't feel safe as they used to.

As I argued, these assumptions are implicitly framed as truth rather than hypothesis. These presuppositions involve ideological attitude (about US foreign policy) so we might argue that local semantics here aims at strengthening consent, at calling on citizens to gather around the ideological square and ultimately at persuading them about the necessity of war.

Admittedly, some critics of the Government's policies are mentioned in the speech and remarked through the use of hendiadys:

Over the hard road of the past months, we have at times met obstacles and difficulties, divisions and disputes, indifference and callousness. That is now all past—and, I am sure, forgotten.

Nevertheless, arguments of opposition or disagreement are not explained or explicitly referred to. The reasons of opponents are left unvoiced and rather given a negative presentation by means of lexical choice: they are defined as «obstacles and difficulties», as something to ride over on the "hard road", «divisions and disputes», as those which threaten national unity, and «indifference and callousness», typical of those who do not hold dear the nation priorities. Thus, opposition to the policies of Government is implicitly regarded as part of the challenge (Axis attacks) that the nation must face, as if anyone who does not agree with the government's policies was outside the national ideological square. Moreover, "all that" is asserted to be past and forgotten, thus conveying a feeling of relief.

So far we have seen in detail how motivations for war are presented and modalized. But what about war's aims and goals? Let us start from an overview of the speech evaluation strategy (Van Dijk 1997: 28). As I have argued, semantic polarization sets positive self-presentation against negative other - presentation: enemies are portrayed as skilful, irrational, unreasonable and calculating people, almost inhuman, compared to a mechanized force, only driven by desires for worldwide conquest. On the other hand, American people are depicted as civilized, fair, rational and peaceful. Thus, if the Axis powers are presented as the aggressors, conversely American people are seen as the victims. This picture seems to prove Robert Ivie's claims, according to which American justification for war usually pivots on contrastive pairs such as force vs. freedom, irrationality vs. rationality and aggression vs. defense, and «warfare is characterized as a means of last resort, a necessary evil forced upon a reluctant nation by the aggressive acts of an enemy bent upon the alienation of humankind from their liberties» (Ivie 1980: 279). In Roosevelt's speech, reluctance to fight is emphasized as much as war's necessity;

We don't like it – we didn't want to get in it – but we are in it and we're going to fight it with everything we've got.

Moral (defence of «common decency») and ideological (defence of «freedom» and «right») motivations are advanced to justify their fight:

Together with other free peoples, we are now fighting to maintain our right to live among our world neighbors in freedom and in common decency, without fear of assault.

Despite Roosevelt's denial («We are now in the midst of a war, not for conquest, not for vengeance»), from the lexical choice it becomes evident that the underlying moral accounting scheme is Revenge (or Retribution) (Lakoff 1995). In fact on closer inspection we notice many expressions which belong to the logic of vengeance: it is said that Japanese danger and shame must be "wiped out", and "eliminated", that only a similar grand strategy can "match" the enemies' strategy, that entering the conflict is a sort of "obligation" to the children of the dead and that the Government is able to administer "proper punishment" to the perpetrators. As Lakoff argues, Revenge accounting scheme creates a moral dilemma: can doing something harmful to those who have done something harmful to us be interpreted as moral? In this particular case: does returning fire against aggressors mean acting immorally or not?

The problem seems to be solved (or eluded) by shifting the focus "above and beyond the ugly field of battle", i.e. from "the immediate evil" to the end of the war and its "ultimate good". In other words, the rationale for entering the war is that the end justifies the means.

The true goal we seek is far above and beyond the ugly field of battle. When we resort to force, as now we must, we are determined that this force shall be directed toward ultimate good as well as against immediate evil.

These statements imply that there is a "good" and "right" use of force and an "evil" one, and they also presuppose that the United States is on the side of right.

We Americans are not destroyers —we are builders. We are now in the midst of a war, not for conquest, not for vengeance, but for a world in which this Nation, and all that this Nation represents, will be safe for our children.

The moral dilemma is expressed clearly by the antithesis at the end of the speech:

"We are going to win the war and we are going to win the peace that follows"

Notice that since "win" is the joining term which connects war and peace, thus winning the war is again presented as the *sine qua non* condition for the survival of the nation and the freedom "under God" of its citizens.

As usual, the American national anthem ends the radio broadcast.

Chapter 4:
GLOSSARY OF RHETORICAL TERMS

A

- **Accumulation.** Figure of speech in which a speaker or writer gathers several points and list them together.
- **Anadiplosis.** Repeating the last word of one clause or phrase to begin the next. E.g. "Watch your 'thoughts, for they will become *actions*. Watch your *actions*, for they'll become... *habits*. Watch your *habits* for they will forge your *character*. Watch your *character*, for it will make your destiny." (Margaret Thatcher in the motion picture *The Iron Lady*).
- **Analogy.** The use of a similar or parallel case or example to reason or argue a point.
- **Anaphora.** From the Greek ἀ ναφέρω, "I repeat". A succession of sentences beginning with the same word or group of words. E.g. "*We shall* not flag or fail. *We shall* go on to the end. *We shall* fight in France, *we shall* fight on the seas and oceans [...]" (Winston Churchill).
- **Anastrophe.** Inversion of the natural word order. For example, the usual English order of subject, object and verb might be changed to object-subject-verb, as in saying "you I like" to mean "I like you.".
- **Anecdote.** A brief narrative describing an interesting or amusing event.
- **Antithesis.** It is used when two opposites or contrasting ideas are introduced in the same sentence, for contrasting effect. E.g. "Love is an ideal thing, marriage a real thing." (Goethe)
- **Antonomasia.** The substitution of an epithet for a proper name. E.g. "The iron lady" for Margaret Thatcher.
- **Aposiopesis.** It is a figure of speech for an unfinished thought or broken sentence. A sentence is deliberately broken off and left unfinished. It can simulate the impression of a speaker so overwhelmed by emotions that he or she is unable to continue speaking. An example would be the threat "Don't do that, or else—!".

- **Apostrophe.** It occurs when a speaker breaks off from addressing the audience. E.g. "My fellow citizens....".
- **Asyndeton.** The deliberate omission of conjunctions that would normally be used. E.g. "He was a bag of bones, a floppy doll, a broken stick, a maniac." (Jack Kerouac, *On the Road*, 1957).

B

- **Bicolon.** A pair of adjacent nouns, adjectives or phrases. E.g. "chop and change", "bag and baggage".

C

- **Captatio benevolentiae.** A rethoric strategy concisting in moving the public to a favourable disposition towards the *rhetor* and his cause.
- **Chiasmus**. From the name of the Greek letter "χ", a figure of speech consisting of the contrasting of two structurally parallel syntactic phrases arranged "cross-wise", i.e. in such a way that the second is in reverse order from the first. For example "One should eat to live, not live to eat" (Cicero).
- **Climax**. It represents a figure of speech, where words, phrases or sentences are placed in an ascending order, according to their importance. E.g. "Let a man acknowledge his obligations to himself, his family, his country, and his God".

E

- **Enumeration.** It is a long, detailed list of objects, places or people.
- **Epanalepsis**. A figure of speech in which the same word or phrase appears both at the beginning and at the end of a clause. E.g. "The king is dead, long live the king".
- **Epiphora**. The repetition of a phrase or word at the end of several sentences or clauses. E.g. "Where affections bear rule, their reason *is subdued*, honesty *is subdued*, good will *is subdued*, and all things else that withstand evil, for ever *are subdued*" (Thomas Wilson).
- **Euphemism**. It is a generally innocuous word or expression used in place of one that may be found offensive or suggest something unpleasant. Some euphemisms are intended to amuse; while others use bland, inoffensive, and often misleading terms for things the user wishes to dissimulate or downplay. Euphemisms are used for dissimulation, to refer to taboo topics (such as disability, sex, excretion, and death) in a polite way. (E.g. To pass away = to die).
- **Exemplum**. The citation of an example, either truthful or fictitious. (Plural: EXEMPLA).

G

- **Gemination.** The immediate repetition of a word, phrase, etc. E.g. "The attack at Pearl Harbor can be repeated at any one of many points, points in both oceans and along both our coast lines and against all the rest of the hemisphere." (Roosevelt).

H

- **Hendiadys**. Using two nouns linked by a conjunction to express a single complex idea. E.g. "with friendship and peace" (instead of "with peaceful friendship").
- **Hyperbole**. It is the use of exaggeration. It may be used to evoke strong feelings or to create a strong impression, but is not meant to be taken literally. E.g. "The bag weighed a ton.".
- **Hypophora**. When a speaker asks aloud what his/her adversaries have to say for themselves or against the speaker, and then proceeds to answer the question.

I

- **Irony**. A deliberate contrast between indirect and direct meaning to draw attention to the opposite. In its broadest sense, is a rhetorical device, literary technique, or event characterized by an incongruity, or contrast, between what the expectations of a situation are and what is really the case, with a third element, that defines that what is really the case is ironic because of the situation that led to it.
- **Isocolon**. A string of phrases of corresponding structure and equal length. "Let each man search his conscience and search his speeches." (Winston Churchill).

J

- **Jargon**. Highly technical language used by specific group.

L

- **Litotes.** Stating a positive by negating the negative. E.g. "You are not as young as you used to be" = You are old.

M

- **Maxim**. A saying drawn from life, which shows concisely either what happens or ought to happen in life, for example: "Every beginning is difficult."
- **Metaphor**. A figure of speech where a word that normally applies to one thing is used to designate another for the sake of creating a mental picture. In simpler terms, a metaphor compares two objects/things without using the words "like" or "as". For example

  All the world's a stage/ And all the men and women merely players/ They have their exits and their entrances (<u>William Shakespeare</u>, <u>*As You Like It*</u>). This quotation contains a metaphor because the world is not literally a stage. By figuratively asserting that the world is a stage, Shakespeare uses the points of comparison between the world and a stage to convey an understanding about the mechanics of the world and the lives of the people within it.
- **Metonymy**. A figure of speech which substitutes one word or phrase for another with which it is closely associated. E. g. "Washington" for the "United States government".

O

- **Onomatopoeia**. Words that imitate the sounds, objects, or actions they refer to. (ex. "buzz", "hullabaloo," "bling").
- **Oxymoron**. A condensed paradox. E.g. "Cold sun".

P

- **Paralipsis**. When a subject is introduced by denying it should be discussed. To speak of someone or something by claiming not to. E.g. "I don't even want to talk about this. Anyway, I can just say that…".
- **Parallelism.** The repetition of similar sentence structures. E.g. "What you see is what you get.".
- **Parenthesis.** An explanatory or qualifying word, clause, or sentence inserted into a passage that is not essential to the literal meaning. E.g. "Billy-bob, *a great singer*, was not a good dancer".
- **Parody**. To imitate something or somebody comically.
- **Periphrasis.** It refers to the use of excessive language and surplus words to convey a meaning that could otherwise be conveyed with fewer words and in more direct a manner. Fori stance: "The big man upstairs hears your prayers" (Refers to God).
- **Personification.** A figure of speech that gives human characteristics to inanimate objects. For example: "The moon played hide and seek with the clouds".
- **Polyptoton**. It is the stylistic scheme in which words derived from the same root are repeated (e.g. "strong" and "strength").
- **Polysyndeton**. The repeated use of conjunctions (usually *and*, *but*, *or*, *nor*) within a sentence, particularly where they are not necessary. E.g. "*And* Joshua, *and* all of Israel with him, took Achan the son of Zerah, *and* the silver, *and* the garment, *and* the wedge of gold, *and* his sons, *and* his daughters, *and* his oxen, *and* his asses, *and* his sheep, *and* his tent, *and* all that he had" (Joshua 7.24).

R

- **Rhetorical question**. A question whose answer may be obvious or immediately provided by the questioner.

S

- **Simile**. A figure of speech that compares unlike things, implying a resemblance between them. For example "Life is like a box of chocolates".
- **Symbol**. A visual or metaphorical representation of an idea or concept.
- **Synecdoche**. There are several different forms of synecdoche examples including:
    - ✓ A synecdoche may use part of something to represent the entire whole.
    - ✓ It may use an entire whole thing to represent a part of it.
    - ✓ It can use a word or phrase as a class that will express less or more than the word or phrase actually means.
    - ✓ It may use a group of things that refer to a larger group or use a large group to refer to a smaller group.
    - ✓ A synecdoche may also refer to an object by the material it is made from or refer to the contents in a container by the name of the container.
- **Synaesthesia**. A process by which one sense modality is described or characterized in terms of another, such as "a bright sound" or "a quiet colour".

T

- **Topos.** A traditional theme or a standardised method of constructing or treating an argument.
- **Tricolon**. The pattern of three phrases in parallel, found commonly in Western writing after Cicero. For example, "Veni, vidi vici".

U

- **Understatement**. A form of irony in which something is represented as less than it really is, with the intent of drawing attention to and emphasizing the opposite meaning.

    Example: "I have to have this operation. It isn't very serious. I have this tiny little tumor on the brain." (Holden Caulfield in *The Catcher In The Rye*, by J. D. Salinger).

Z

- **Zeugma.** A figure of speech in which one word applies to two others in different senses of that word, and in some cases only logically applies to one of the other two words. E.g., "Kill the boys and the luggage!" (Fluellen in William Shakespeare's Henry V).